Basic Keyboarding

SECOND EDITION

Skills and Applications for Computers and Typewriters

Rodney G. Jurist • Lyn Tisdale

D1410894

The H. M. Rowe Company
Baltimore

Essential Skills and Applications in One Semester!

We gratefully acknowledge the review and testing contributions of many teachers and their students, including these students at ICM School of Business: Jesse Behe, Renee Bergia, Brian Carson, Leah King, Jane McGrane, Jeff McKivens, Loverta Miller, Kelley Milligan, and Rose Moore. We especially thank these instructors for their work:

Kathleen C. Cain
ICM School of Business
Pittsburgh, Pennsylvania

James Trick
Williamsport School of Commerce
Williamsport, Pennsylvania

Editorial Assistance: Kristen Cassereau
                      Maureen McCafferty
                      Charles Raymond

Basic Keyboarding, Second Edition

List No. 180-2 ■ ISBN 0-88294-346-4 ■ 9702-2

The H. M. Rowe Company
624 North Gilmor Street • Baltimore, MD 21217
Toll-free orders: 1-800-638-6026   Fax: (410) 728-7709

Whether you are a student or an employee, you have a lot of demands on your time. You need to develop a new skill or review an old skill in the shortest time possible. *Basic Keyboarding, Second Edition*, is designed with your goals *and* your timetable in mind.

This is a one-semester course in keyboarding skills and essential applications. Because these are *essential* applications, you'll find an emphasis on basic formats. You'll notice a focus on keyboarding speed and accuracy throughout the book. Finally, you'll find lessons devoted to proofreading and rough drafts.

When this course ends, you should be able to

- Keyboard at 50 words per minute with high accuracy

- Find errors in your copy (proofread)

- Judge when a document appearance is acceptable, even if you've never prepared a particular form before

- Make corrections in a document

- Use fonts to enhance the impact of your work

- Prepare letters, memos, tables, and reports with confidence

You can complete your work at a computer or a typewriter. The only rule to remember is the one shown above—*every lesson counts*. Don't expect to find all the answers in the book. Be prepared to use the knowledge and experience gained in the early lessons to complete the assignments toward the end.

As you probably know, one of the essential aspects of any skill is the ability to ask good questions and find acceptable answers. You will be developing that skill in this course as you learn to keyboard and format with confidence.

If you make every lesson count, you will get results with *Basic Keyboarding*!

EQUIPMENT   *Parts and Functions*

Know Your Equipment. Read about both kinds of equipment—typewriters and computers—on the following pages. You will often be expected to switch from one kind of machine to another.

MARK	EXAMPLE	MEANING
℘	I talks to the home office.	take out
/	I talk to the home office.	change
⌒	I ta lk to the home office.	close up
℘	I talk to the hoome office.	take out, close up
∧	I talk to ^the home office.	insert
#	I talk#to the home office.	add space
⌃	Yes, I talk to the home office.	add comma
⊙	I talk to the home office⊙	add period
⌒	I talk the to home office.	reverse order
⌐	⌐I talk to the home office.	move left
⌐	⌐I talk to the home office.	move right
⌐ ⌐	⌐Home Office⌐	center
¶	¶Home Office systems are new.	new paragraph
⌒	I talked to the home office. They are sending the manuals.	run in
≡	Address mail to home Office.	capitalize
/	Did you call my Extension?	lowercase
◯ sp	We have offices throughout the U.S.	spell out
◯→	Bring paper, a pencil, and the text.	move
⋯⋯	Bring a pencil, paper, and the text.	stet (leave as is)

In general, computers have had a good effect on document quality. However, the convenience of computers makes it all the easier to miss mistakes. Built-in checking features cannot substitute for your own proofreading. Learn to proofread, and check every document you produce for accuracy.

If you have time, read a document twice. The first time, check for sense (is all information there? do the numbers make sense?). The second time, check for typos, punctuation errors, and format mistakes.

Don't try to read too quickly. Avoid distractions when you proofread.

Check these potential trouble spots carefully:

1. Spelling of proper names.

2. Spelling and capitalization of words in inside address, salutation, and complimentary close.

3. Spelling of headings and words in capital letters.

4. Spelling of words that can be easily confused with other words, such as *to* and *too*.

5. Spelling of words that become other words if misspelled, such as *quite* and *quiet*.

Be sure you understand the name and function of every part shown.

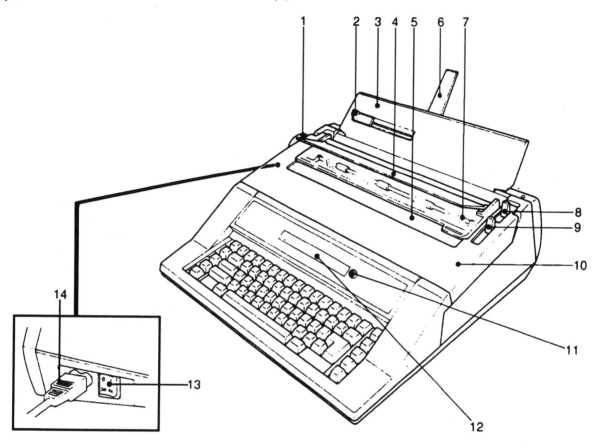

1. **Platen Knob**
   Allows manual rotation of platen.

2. **Paper Guide**
   Provides for consistent paper placement.

3. **Paper Support (Paper Table)**
   Supports paper during typing or printing.

4. **Glare Shield**
   Protects typing line from direct light.

5. **Margin Scale**
   Numerical indicator for carrier position.

6. **Page End Indicator**
   Supports paper and indicates remaining paper length (inches, for 11" paper).

7. **Noise Cover**
   Buffers the sound of typing or printing.

8. **Paper Release Lever**
   Releases paper for alignment.

9. **Paper Bail Lever**
   Lifts bail; may provide automatic paper insertion.

10. **Top Cover**
    Opens for replacement of accessories.

11. **Contrast Control**
    Adjusts the display for easier reading.

12. **Adjustable Display**
    Displays typed characters.

13. **Power Switch**
    Turns power on and off.

14. **Power Cord**
    Supplies power to machine.

Use figures for the time with *a.m.* and *p.m.* Spell out the number with *o'clock*:

I arrived at 8 a.m.
Call for a cab at 5:30 p.m.
We close at five o'clock.

Do not separate a figure from *a.m.* or *p.m.* at the end of the line. Also, don't separate the month from the day. (On a computer, use a *hard space* to prevent a bad line break between the number and the units.)

According to our plan, the party will be on July 25 at 7:30 p.m. (don't break *July* and *25* or *7:30* and *p.m.*)

Use figures when writing the full date:

January 1, 19-- (not *January 1st, 19--*)

When writing dollar amounts, insert a comma every three places from the dollar column. Use a period for the decimal point for amounts with cents:

$43,110 $33.45

If some dollar amounts in a sentence include cents, all amounts should include cents. Add zeros to the amounts without cents:

Their expenses totaled $396.50 and $95.00, respectively.

COMMAS

Use a comma to separate three or more items in a series:

We ordered sandwiches, fries, and sodas.
Jane, Marita, and I went to New York.

Use a comma between descriptive words (adjectives) if the word *and* could be naturally inserted between them:

I admire your calm, considerate attitude.

Don't use a comma after *but* or *and* in sentences like these:

Kay wanted to attend, but she made other plans. (not *Kay wanted to attend but, she made other plans.*)

Use a comma to separate independent clauses joined by *and* or *but*. (Clause: part of a sentence that contains a verb form.)

The report is complete, and we have scheduled a meeting on February 19 for general discussion.

Mr. Goldstein called, but he didn't leave a message.

Use commas to set off words of direct address:

Joanne, please take this call.
I'll let you know, Chris, when the books arrive.

Use commas to set off city names with state names and to set off parts of the full date:

Have you ever visited Dallas, Texas?
I visited Dallas, Texas, on May 9, 1992.
June 4, 1991, was my graduation day.

Use a comma to set off introductory words in a sentence, including clauses that are moved to the beginning of the sentence:

Yes, we would very much like to participate.
Even though you called, I still expected a note.

Use a comma to set off a contrasting expression:

I ordered these items in white, not blue.

OTHER PUNCTUATION

Use a period at the end of a sentence. (*Note:* A sentence never begins with *but*.) Be sure your sentence includes a *subject* and a *predicate*. In this example, the subject is shown in italics and the predicate is underlined:

David <u>took the test yesterday</u>.

Use an apostrophe to show possession:

That looks like Peter's notebook.
Please don't eat the children's dinner.
The dog ate its food. (No apostrophe for a possessive pronoun. This is a common error.)

Use an apostrophe in a contraction where a letter or letters have been omitted:

I can't seem to understand the new program.

These parts (or parts that function like them) are under the top cover. Check your manual to find the parts that perform the functions listed below. ■ *Note:* Except for routine ribbon changes, do not attempt to adjust any elements inside the machine.

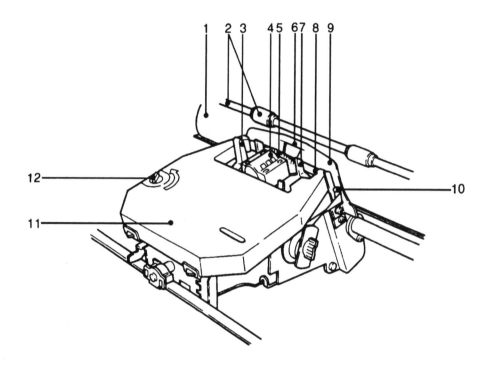

1. **Platen**
   Rolls paper in and out.

2. **Paper Bail and Bail Rollers**
   Holds paper against platen.

3. **Printwheel Release Lever**
   Pulls forward for replacing print wheel.

4. **Hammer**
   Strikes print wheel.

5. **Print Wheel**
   Contains all letters and characters in font.

6. **Print Point Indicator**
   Indicates print position.

7. **Ribbon Guide**
   Guides ribbon across print point.

8. **Correction Tape**
   Allows automatic correction of errors.

9. **Card Holder**
   Holds index card or other card against the platen for typing.

10. **Guide Roller**
    Guides correction tape across print point.

11. **Ribbon Cassette**
    Holds ribbon (normally single-use ribbon).

12. **Ribbon Take-Up Knob**
    Allows manual tightening of ribbon.

ordinarily	programming	satisfactory	though
organization	prominent	schedule	thorough
pamphlet	pronounce	scissors	through
parallel	pronunciation	secretary	tomorrow
partial	prosecute	separate	traceable
particular	psychology	sergeant	transferable
patience	publicity	serviceable	transferred
patients	publicly	significant	turnaround
peculiar	pursue	similar	typing
Pennsylvania	pursuing	simultaneous	undoubtedly
permanent	quantity	sincerely	unforeseen
permissible	realtor	specialize	unnecessary
persistent	receipt	specialty	until
personnel	receivable	specifically	unusual
persuade	receivership	sponsor	unwieldy
phenomenal	recipient	statistics	usage
piece	recognize	strength	valuable
possession	recommend	strict	variable
practically	recurrence	strictly	vehicle
precede	reference	substantial	villain
preferable	referring	succeed	volume
preferred	reimbursement	sufficient	Wednesday
preparation	relieve	superintendent	weight
privilege	resistance	surprise	whether
procedure	resource	susceptible	wholly
proceed	reunion	technique	witness
processor	ridiculous	telecommunication	wraparound
professional	salary	terminal	yield

QUICK REFERENCE — English Review

CAPITAL LETTERS

Capitalize the names of people. (Some last names include capital letters within the name.)

John Williams   **Susan R. McDonald**

Capitalize the names of specific places:

I grew up in St. Paul, Minnesota.
Her address is 18 Harbor Square.
Have you visited the Midwest?

Capitalize courtesy and professional titles:

Ms. Joleen Summers
Dr. George Mantero
Victor Wu, M.D.

Capitalize only the first word in the complimentary close of a letter:

Sincerely yours

Capitalize the first word and all important words in the title of a book or other publication:

Using Your Personal Computer (book)
"Europe on a Budget" (article)

NUMBERS

Spell out whole numbers between one and ten:

I sent ten copies to you today.
Press the Enter key four times.

This is a typical typewriter keyboard. Check your manual to find the keys that perform the following functions on your equipment.

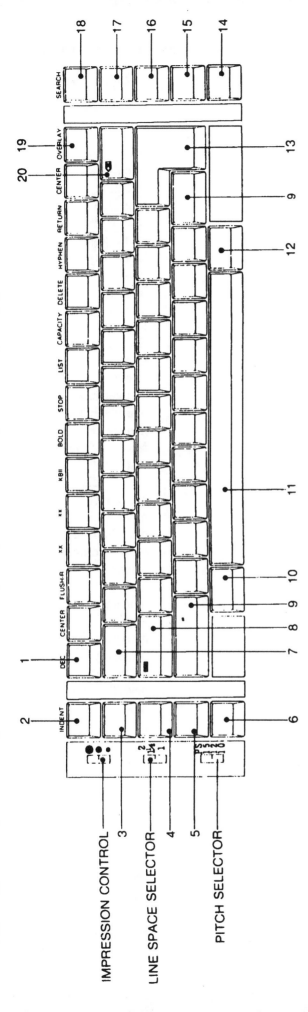

1. **Margin Release**
   Releases margins for typing or moving carriage beyond them.

2. **Left Margin**
   Sets the left margin at print point.

3. **Right Margin**
   Sets the right margin at print point.

4. **Tab Set/Clear**
   Sets and clears tabs.

5. **Mode Key**
   Changes typewriter processing function.

6. **Code Key**
   Activates special functions when used with other keys.

7. **Tab/Back Tab Key**
   Moves carrier or cursor to the next tab setting (ahead or previous).

8. **Shift Lock Key**
   Locks Shift to give all capital letters (releases when a Shift Key is pressed).

9. **Shift Key**
   Allows typing of capital letters and of symbols in top row.

10. **Repeat Key**
    Repeats the last key or function typed.

11. **Space Bar**
    Moves carrier or cursor ahead one space. (Repeats if held down.)

12. **Half-Space Key**
    Moves the carrier ahead ½ space.

13. **Return Key**
    Returns carrier or cursor to beginning of next line.

14. **Print Key**
    Prints text shown in display (also prints file stored in memory).

15. **Reverse Index Key**
    Rolls paper backward ½ line (1/12") without moving carrier. (Repeats if held down.)

16. **Index Key**
    Advances paper forward 1/2 line (1/12") without moving carrier. (Repeats if held down.)

17. **Relocation Key**
    Moves carrier one space to right of last character typed on page. (On display, moves cursor one space to right of last character in line or file.)

18. **Express Key**
    Returns the carrier to the left margin on the current line.

19. **Backspace Key**
    Moves carrier or cursor one space to the left. (Repeats if held down.)

20. **Correction Key**
    Automatically deletes character or characters printed or displayed to left of print point. (Repeats if held down.)

WORDS OFTEN MISSPELLED

abbreviate	cancel	dissatisfied	intelligent
absence	capability	efficient	intention
absolutely	cassette	eligible	intercede
accessible	changeable	eliminate	interference
accessory	character	embarrass	knowledge
accidentally	collateral	emphasize	laboratory
accommodate	commission	encouragement	leisure
accompanying	commitment	enforceable	length
accrued	committee	enthusiastic	liaison
accumulate	competent	equipment	library
accuracy	comptroller	equipped	license
accustom	concede	especially	likable
achieve	conceivable	essential	likely
acknowledge	conference	exaggerate	maintenance
acquaint	conscientious	exercise	manageable
acquitted	conscious	expense	manual
across	consensus	experience	Massachusetts
administrative	consequently	explanation	mathematics
advantageous	convenient	extension	merchandise
advisable	correspondence	extraordinary	messenger
alignment	correspondents	familiar	mileage
alleged	courageous	fascinating	miscellaneous
allotment	criticize	February	misdemeanor
allotted	currency	foreign	Mississippi
amendment	deceive	foresee	misspell
analysis	decision	forfeit	monetary
analyze	deductible	formatting	monitor
apparent	defense	forty	mortgage
applicant	deficit	fourth	necessary
approximately	definite	freight	negotiate
argument	depreciate	friend	nevertheless
associate	descend	fulfill	ninety
athletics	describe	government	ninth
attacked	description	grammar	noticeable
attendance	desirable	grievance	numeric
authoritative	desperate	guidance	oblige
autumn	develop	harass	obsolete
auxiliary	differed	height	occasion
bankruptcy	dilemma	illegible	occupant
believed	dimension	imitation	occurred
beneficiary	disappear	immediate	occurrence
bookkeeper	disappoint	incidentally	offered
budget	disastrous	incur	official
bulletin	disbursement	independent	omission
business	discrepancy	indispensable	opportunity
calendar	discretion	initiative	opposite

The function keys within parentheses apply to WordPerfect® 5.0/5.1. If you are using a later version of WordPerfect® (6.0 or higher), or if you are using other software, check your manual for the correct procedures and fill in the correct steps for your software. You might want to make a set of index cards for quick reference.

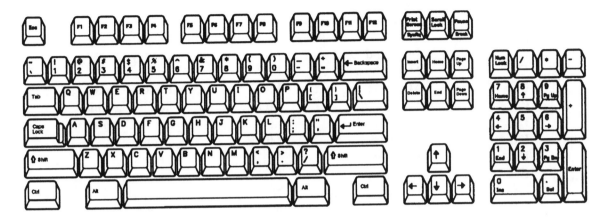

1. **Cancel (F1)**
   Cancels previous step (allows restoring of deleted copy).

2. **Help (F3)**
   Gives on-line help for software features.

3. **Reveal Codes (Alt–F3 or F11)**
   Shows codes at current position in document.

4. **Indent (F4)**
   Indents left margin to next tab setting until hard return is keyed.

5. **List Files (F5)**
   Lists stored files in default directory for retrieval, printing, or copying.

6. **Bold (F6)**
   Makes type print darker for emphasis. Press again or use right arrow key to turn off bold.

7. **Center (Shift–F6)**
   Turns on centering. Hard return turns off.

8. **Exit (F7)**
   Exits word processing; returns to DOS.

9. **Print (Shift–F7)**
   Gives access to print menu (choices).

10. **Underline (F8 Key)**
    Turns on underscore. Press again or use right arrow key to turn off underline.

11. **Format (Shift–F8)**
    Gives access to various line, page, and print format menus (choices).

12. **Font (Ctrl–F8)**
    Gives access to various font (type) choices and features.

13. **Graphics (Alt–F9)**
    Allows access to various features such as text boxes and equations.

14. **Save (F10)**
    Saves current file for later retrieval. (File name can include up to 8 characters and a 3–character extension, such as MORGAN.LTR.)

15. **Retrieve (Shift–F10)**
    Allows quick retrieval of a file.

16. **Escape Key**
    Cancels the current operation.

17. **Delete Key**
    Deletes character at cursor position.

18. **Backspace Key (←)**
    Deletes character preceding cursor.

19. **Cursor Keys (↑, →, ↓, ←)**
    Move cursor through text on screen.

20. **Insert Key**
    Allows typing of new copy over existing copy.

STATE AND TERRITORY ABBREVIATIONS

Alabama	AL	Kentucky	KY	Ohio	OH
Alaska	AK	Louisiana	LA	Oklahoma	OK
Arizona	AZ	Maine	ME	Oregon	OR
Arkansas	AR	Maryland	MD	Pennsylvania	PA
California	CA	Massachusetts	MA	Puerto Rico	PR
Colorado	CO	Michigan	MI	Rhode Island	RI
Connecticut	CT	Minnesota	MN	South Carolina	SC
Delaware	DE	Mississippi	MS	South Dakota	SD
District of Columbia	DC	Missouri	MO	Tennessee	TN
Florida	FL	Montana	MT	Texas	TX
Georgia	GA	Nebraska	NE	Utah	UT
Guam	GU	Nevada	NV	Vermont	VT
Hawaii	HI	New Hampshire	NH	Virgin Islands	VI
Idaho	ID	New Jersey	NJ	Virginia	VA
Illinois	IL	New Mexico	NM	Washington	WA
Indiana	IN	New York	NY	West Virginia	WV
Iowa	IA	North Carolina	NC	Wisconsin	WI
Kansas	KS	North Dakota	ND	Wyoming	WY

HOW TO FOLD A LETTER

1 shows a No. 10 envelope; 2 shows a 6¾ envelope; 3 shows a window envelope

KEYBOARDING ESSENTIALS

1. Locate Power Switch

Locate the power switch for your equipment. Turn on the power. You will hear a beep, and you may see an indicator light showing that power is now on.

2. Insert Paper

At a computer, follow the instructions in your manual to feed paper into the printer or fill the paper tray for automatic feed.

At a typewriter, set the paper guide to 0. Pull the paper bail forward. Holding the paper against the paper guide with your left hand, lower the edge evenly behind the cylinder. Now press the Index Key to advance the paper *or* turn the cylinder knob with your right hand, using a twisting motion to pull the paper into the machine. When the paper is in place, lower the paper bail onto the surface of the cylinder.

Note: Get into the habit of using the Index Key (and the Reverse Index Key) to move the paper forward or back. (Do not use the platen knob.) The memory correction feature will not work properly if you use the knob.

3. Change Paper Position

(Typewriter) You may need to move the paper slightly after it has been inserted. If so, pull the paper release forward. Only the paper bail is now holding the paper in place. Move the paper carefully as desired and reset the paper release.

4. Remove Paper

(Typewriter) Pull the paper bail forward. Pull the paper release forward and remove the paper. Return the paper release to its original position.

5. Set Type Pitch

The pitch is the type size. The pitch number refers to the number of characters that fit horizontally in 1 inch. In a typewriter font, each character takes the same amount of space. Your machine may offer proportional spacing, in which the letters are given only the amount of space needed. Dot matrix and laser printers

Apex

Computer Hotline Service
100 Corporate Plaza
Tulsa, OK 74102-8890
1-800-555-APEX

May 7, 19--

Ms. Jane Jackson, Personnel Administrator
University Hospital
1550 Westside Ave.
Fairfield, NJ 07080-1145

Dear Ms. Jackson:

It is our pleasure to inform you of an important change in
Apex Computer Hotline Service. As you know, Apex
Computers provides this service to all our customers to
ensure ~~the~~ immediate and ~~most~~ efficient support with any
hardware or software problem that may arise. Now ~~that~~ *our*
service will be even more efficient ~~due to~~ *with* our new Triage
Program.

~~Please inform your computer operators and their~~ *(the Apex)*
~~supervisors that now~~ when you call ~~our~~ hotline your call
will be answered <u>immediately</u>. No more long waits! Your
problem will be assessed by a trained technician who will
route your call to the appropriate computer support person.
~~for you.~~ We realize there were difficulties and
frustrations with our former procedure but, we are working
to improve our service. we know we have done so with this
important change.

Billing and other service arrangements remain the same. *Please*
call if you need further info.

Sincerely,

Bill James
Vice President
Customer Service

rmt

---

2 ■ *Form 20-2* ■ *Key this letter with the corrections shown.* ■
Find the errors that were missed. ■ *Proofread your own work.*

3 ■ *Form 20-3* ■ *Write a short memo from Mr. James to Anne
Collins.* ■ *Use the standard format.* ■ *Proofread and correct
all errors before submitting complete project.*

offer a variety of fonts (type styles). Printer fonts are measured either in points or in characters per inch (cpi). The standard size for text in a laser font is 11 or 12 points.

Fonts. On a typewriter, change the print wheel and pitch setting to match the font. These fonts are often available:

```
This is what your equipment prints when you select
10-pitch (10 cpi) type.  Note that each letter
takes up the same amount of space on the line.
This is called a monospace (one space) font because
of the even spacing for each letter.        (10-cpi Courier)
```

```
This is 12-pitch (12 cpi) type.  Note how you can fit more
words to a line than in 10-pitch type.  Each letter still
occupies the same amount of space.         (12-cpi Courier)
```

This is a font called Times Roman. It is commonly available on many laser printers. If you can't find Times on your list of laser printer fonts, you can find something like it. Note how many words can fit on a standard line. Also, note that the letters don't occupy the same amount of space. This is a *proportional* font. You can learn more about fonts in Lesson 44.

(Times Roman, 11 point—laser printer)

This is another common proportional font called Univers. If you can't find Univers on your list of laser printer fonts, you can find something like it. Note that this font "sets bigger" than Times Roman, and therefore it takes more space on the line.

(Universe, 11 point—laser printer)

The standard setting for most word processing software is 10 cpi.

6. Know Paper Dimensions

Standard typing paper is 8½ inches wide and 11 inches long. Continuous-feed paper (dot matrix printers) and laser printer paper also measures 8½ by 11 inches. (At a computer, the screen page is the same size as your standard-size piece of paper.) You should know the width of the paper (and your screen, if appropriate) in **spaces** and the length in **line spaces.**

In 10-pitch type, 1 inch = 10 spaces. Therefore, 8½ inches equals 85 spaces across in 10-pitch type. In 12-pitch type, 1 inch = 12 spaces. Therefore, 8½ inches equals 102 spaces across in 12-pitch type.

For most applications, every vertical inch = 6 lines of copy. Therefore, a standard 11-inch-long page (or a page on your computer display) is 66 lines long.

M ◆ E ◆ M ◆ O

To: Bill Reynolds, Vice President
From: Anne Collins, Support Specialist
Date: March 17, 19--
Subject: Improved Handling of Holine Calls

to ~~~ Over the past three years, I have noticed that many customers
wait 15/20 minutes before reaching an operator on our *(wait occurs)*
customer service hotline. This ~~is often~~ because all calls go
directly to our most experienced staff. These calls take
time because ~~it often takes~~ the customer *has* ~~a long time~~ to
explain his/her problem. Meanwhile, customers with actual
emergencies are left to wait or unable to get through.

                    that   *should*
I suggest, all calls, be answered immediately by a few people
whose ~~job it~~ would ~~be to~~ assess the difficulty of the
customer's problem. These people would then route the call
to the appropriate support person. Actual emergencies would *procedure*
receive top priority and be answered immediately This, would
kept ~~~ eliminate much of our customers' frustrations, ~~since~~ they
would not be waiting 15 minutes to have their calls answered
and it would be handled by the ablest person when they do
reach an operator.

We could cover this change by adding to the hours of our
part-time staff. A plan like this might work:

Employee
~~Person~~   Current   Added   Total
     Tom
~~Tim~~ Rainey   25   5   ~~35~~ 30
Rachel Fay   18   15   23
Marcy Richards   20   10   30
Paula Ambrose   21   8   29
Charles Wila   12   15   25

I can provide more information if this sounds sensible to
you.

1 ■ *Form 20-1* ■ *Anne is giving this memo to her boss and
wants it to make a good impression.* ■ *Key the memo with the
corrections marked.* ■ *Correct the 10 errors Anne missed.* ■
Use the standard memo format (see page 80 for review).

7. Set Margins

Computer. Your word processing software includes standard (or default) margin settings. Normally the left margin is set at 1 inch in and the right margin is also set at 1 inch. (The line is 6½ inches long.) These settings are acceptable for all practices in Levels 1 and 2.

Electronic typewriter. Use the Margin Release Key to space past the existing margin (if necessary) and move to a point 1 inch from the left edge of the paper (10 spaces for 10-pitch type; 12 spaces for 12-pitch type). Press the **left margin key.** Then move to the right edge of the sheet and press the **right margin key.**

Electric or manual typewriter. Move the printing point to 10 and position the **left margin stop** at that point. To set the right margin, move the **right margin stop** to the far right side. Use the **line gauge** as a guide.

8. Set Vertical Spacing

Most exercises in this book are set up for **single-spacing.** Set your equipment for single-spacing.

The **line space regulator** sets the number of vertical spaces between lines of type. In **single-spacing,** the second typed line begins 1 line space below the first typed line. There is no blank line between typed lines. The lines of this paragraph are single-spaced.

In **double-spacing,** the second typed line begins 2 line spaces below the first

typed line. There is 1 blank line between typed lines. The lines of this

paragraph are shown in double-spacing.

If you are using a **computer,** check your preset line spacing. If your equipment is set for double-spacing, change the setting to single-spacing. (See page 4 for computer keys and functions.)

9. Look at Copy

Once you learn the keyboard, never watch your fingers as you work. Complete extra practice (see Levels 1 and 2) if you find yourself looking at the keys often.

July 11, 19--

Mr. James Randolph
Anderson Technologies
75 Wilson ~~Drive~~ *Avenue*
Paradise, CA 95969-7421

Dear Mr. Randolf:

I am writing in response to ~~you~~ *your* ad in <u>The Portland Times</u>
about the administrative assistant position available in
the Accounting Department at Anderson Technologies.

~~As you can see from my resume,~~ I am currently employed in
the Accounts Payable Office at Portland community
Hospital. In this position I have had more than two years *of*
experience handling complicated billing forms. I am
responsible for initiating the billing process, verifying *all*
insurance information, and entering information into our *and 6.0*
computer system. I am proficient with WordPerfect 5.1 and ....
with DataPlan. ~~These are~~ skills ~~I know~~ ~~would~~ *will* be of value at
Anderson Technologies. *(I hope these)*

I am very interested in the administrative assistant
position ~~available~~ advertised, *and* I would appreciate an
opportunity to be interviewed. I can arrange to visit
Anderson Technologies at your convenience and would gladly
relocate. *to pursue this opportunity.*

Sincerely,

Marie McDermot
99-14 Whitecap Street
Portland, OR 97205-0011
(503) 555-1442

---

2 ■ *Form 19-2* ■ *Key this application cover letter with the
corrections shown.* ■ *Find the 3 proper noun errors that Marie
missed.* ■ *Proofread your own work. (Getting an interview can
depend on an error-free cover letter.)*

Calculating Speed

For calculating keyboarding or typing speed, 5 characters (including spaces) = 1 word. The timing exercises in this course include a scale that looks like this:

```
This is a 10-word line.  The Return (or Space) is
the last character on the line for a total of 50.
--1----2----3----4----5----6----7----8----9---10--
```

If you keyboard these two lines in **1 minute**, you have typed 20 standard words. Your speed is 20 words per minute. If you keyboard these two lines in **30 seconds**, you have typed 40 words per minute (multiply the time x 2 to get 1 minute, and multiply the number of words typed x 2).

To save time and work later on, concentrate on accuracy. If you have 5 or more errors, retake the timing at a slower rate. For up to 4 errors, subtract 1 word from your rate for each error. For example, if you typed 45 words per minute (wpm) with 3 errors, your rate is 45 − 3 = 42 wpm.

If you are a beginner, your rate will probably start out under 30 words per minute. Aim for a good production rate of 50 words per minute by the end of this course.

Finding Errors

Types of common errors are listed below. (*Note:* If a word includes more than 1 error, count only 1 error. Do not add up every error in the word.)

- Letters out of order (*teh* for *the*)
- Letter doubled (*wantt* for *want*)
- Letter or space omitted (*repot* for *report*)
- Extra space after word (*one   I* for *one I*)
- Incorrect punctuation (*U.S,* for *U.S.*)
- Wrong case (*PATENT Office* for *Patent Office*)
- Incorrect spacing (incorrect tab, margin, or "hard" return)
- Word omitted (*revise first* for *revise the first*)
- Words transposed (*go can* for *can go*)

Can you find every mistake in the sample below? Proofreading skill and error correction practice can save you time and help you build speed. (Proofreaders' marks are shown on page 107.)

```
I do not wantt to write a new repot to explain teh
one   I received yesterday.  The U.S, PATENT Office
sentus the correct forms last week.  I hope we go
can ahead and revise first report.
```

Marie McDermott
99-14 Whitecap Street
Portland, OR 97205-0011
(503) 555-1442

EDUCATION

1991-1993   Portland Community Colege
                   Associate Degree, Business

1987-~~1991~~   Bayview High School
                   Business Course
                   Accounting courses, A average
                   Word Processing courses, A average

EXPERIENCE

1991-present   Portland Community Hospital
                   Accounts Payable Office
                   Responsibilities: initiate billing for
                   newly admitted patience; operate computer
                   terminal; check all insurance information;
                   maintain office records; prepare daily
                   memos using WordPerfect 5.1 *and* 6.0

1988-1990   Christine's Dress Shop
                   Responsibilities: kept floor stocked;
                   helped customers; worked cash register;
                   provided cash returns for custumers.

REFERENCES

Ms. Thelma Cortez, ~~Instructor~~ *Associate Professor*
Portland Community College
Portland, OR 97205-5572
(503) 682-~~6433~~ *6430*

Mr. Michael Kingston, Manager
Christines Dress Shop
Portland, OR 97204-7298
(503) 684-7222

Mr. Steven Osler, Busness Chair
Bayview High School
Portland, OR 97209
(503) 992-3737

---

1 ▪ *Plain sheet* ▪ *Your friend has asked you to key her resume for a job she really wants.* ▪ *Make the corrections as marked.* ▪ *Correct 5 additional spelling errors.* ▪ *Add boldface and other features as desired to improve appearance.*

1
LEARN THE KEYBOARD

In Level 1, you learn how to keyboard (or type) by touch. You won't have to look at the keyboard because you will memorize the location of the keys.

If You Can Keyboard

If you already know how to type (keyboard), use these lessons for review. If you have never taken a typing class, you are a "hunt-and-peck" typist. If so, give extra attention to these early units. Complete every drill, and check your work carefully for errors. You will succeed in keyboarding by touch, and you will be surprised at the amount of time you save by learning these methods.

Steps for Results

Follow these guidelines for *maximum* results as you complete the lessons in this section:

1. Don't skip lessons or drills. Each has been designed to develop skills.

2. Aim for maximum speed with accuracy—100% accuracy is not too high to aim!

3. Concentrate. If your mind is not on your work, you are not memorizing these simple procedures.

4. Read directions carefully. In each lesson, keyboard each practice line or group of lines twice with single-spacing.

5. Use a manual Return at the end of each practice line, unless your instructor tells you otherwise. The exercise lines are designed to end evenly. This feature helps you to find errors in your work.

With concentration and adequate class time, you might be able to master the keyboard in just 2 weeks!

Preparing an invoice ■ An invoice is a special business form used for billing customers. Even if you have never seen an invoice before, you can readily prepare one for this job by using your experience with tabs and proofreading.

■ If one or more money amounts in a column show cents, all amounts must show cents. ■ Use the left margin for the first column (flush left). ■ Use a ruler or line space counter to measure the space in the preformatted column. Then center the column within this space. ■ Allow at least two spaces to the right of a right tab before the next column begins.

2 ■ *Form 18-2* ■ *Prepare this invoice.* ■ *On a computer, try creating your own form.*

FLOWERS GALORE

INVOICE

85 Richmond Avenue
Portland, OR 97220-2364
(503) 555-4672

DATE May ~~15~~ 14, 19--   *INVOICE NO.* 4722X

TO   Ms. Jennifer Seldon   *BILL TO*   same
       50 Chestnut ~~Lane~~ *Drive*
       Portland, OR 97220-~~2364~~ *1433*

Description	Qty.	Price	Total
Church order--lilies	50	$ 2.50	$125.00
Bride's bouquet--yellow roses	1	45.00	45.00
Maid-of-honor's bouquet--yellow roses	1	30.00	30.00
Bridesmaids' bouquet--yellow roses	3	20.00	60.00
Groom's boutonniere	1	10.00	10.00
Ushers' boutonniere	3	5.00	15.00
		Subtotal	$285.00
		10% Sales Tax	28.50
Best wishes on your happy occasion!		**TOTAL**	$313.50

You read about keyboarding and about your equipment in the introduction. Now you can begin using your machine to keyboard or type basic copy.

Home Keys

When you keyboard, your fingers will be held in position over the Home Keys. The Home Keys are shaded on the keyboard below. The Enter (Return) Key and Space Bar are also shaded.

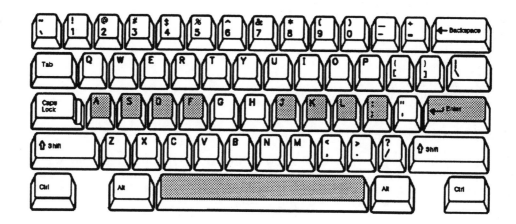

Left Hand	Right Hand
A ■ Use little finger	**J** ■ Use first finger
S ■ Use third finger	**K** ■ Use second finger
D ■ Use second finger	**L** ■ Use third finger
F ■ Use first finger	**;** ■ Use little finger
	Return ■ Use ; finger
	Space ■ Use right thumb

The **Space Bar** is used to insert spaces between words and sentences.

The **Return** or **Enter** Key is used to move to the beginning of the next line of type. On a computer, the Enter Key may show an arrow that goes down and turns left: ↵.

Technique Development

Keyboarding technique is important. Follow these guides every time you type.

■   Sit comfortably at approximately eight inches from the keyboard with both feet on the floor. Your back and shoulders should be straight. Your body should be centered in line with the **H** key.

**FLOWERS
GALORE**

85 Richmond Avenue
Portland, OR 97220-2364
(503) 555-4672

May ~~15~~ 14, 19--

Ms. Jennifer Seldon ,
50 Chestnut ~~Lane~~ Drive
Portland, OR 97220-~~2364~~ 1433

Dear Ms. S⁀eldon

Thank you for placing the flower order for your wedding with
Flowers Galore. We realize what a special occasion this is
and we will do everything we can to ensure that your flowers
are part of the day's ~~success.~~ happiness

on Saturday, June 4. As we discussed, today by phone lilies will be delivered to the Huntington church by
3 p.m. Your bouquet the bouquets for the bridesmaids, as well
as the boutonnieres for the ushers will be delivered to your
mother's house by 2:30 p.m. ¶Best wishes for the special
occasion. at 301 Wells Road

Sincerely

Judy Michaels
Manager

---

1 ■ *Form 18-1* ■ *Key this letter with the corrections
shown.* ■ *Find the 2 comma errors Ms. Michaels
missed.*

■ *To review Proofreaders' Marks, see page 107.*

■ Reach your right hand forward to hover over the Home Keys **J K L ;**. Move your left hand to hover over the Home Keys **A S D F**. Let your fingers curl naturally, and keep your wrists level—do not rest your wrists or hands on the desk or on the keyboard.

Now prepare to keyboard:

1. Turn on the power to your equipment.

2. Be sure your margins will allow you to type a 50-character line. On an electric or electronic typewriter, move the right margin out of the way. On a computer, the standard right margin setting of your software should be acceptable.

3. Insert a standard full-size sheet of paper (8½ x 11 inches) into your typewriter. The top of the sheet should align with the indicator just below the printing point. (If you are using a computer with a dot matrix or laser printer, skip this step. Be sure the printer is on.)

4. Press the Return Key of your typewriter 7 times to leave a top margin of 6 blank lines—1 inch. (Your computer software probably sets a top margin automatically. Check with your instructor if you are not sure.)

New Key Drill

Use a straight-down motion of the finger to tap each key. Make this motion without moving your arm or the rest of your hand.

```
j jj jjj a aa aaa l ll lll d dd ddd   Return
f ff fff k kk kkk s ss sss ; ;; ;;;   Return twice

jjj jjj aaa aaa lll lll ddd ddd jjj   Return
fff fff kkk kkk sss sss ;;; ;;; fff   Return twice

jjj aaa lll ddd jal jal all lad dad   Return
fff kkk sss ;;; fal fad sad dad add   Return twice
```

Accuracy Development

Keyboard the following practice. Remember, keep your fingers curled to tap *straight down* on the Home Keys. Tap just hard enough to make the letter appear on the paper or on the screen.

```
jj ad jad; dad; kad; fad; add; lad; jad; dad; fad

ff ad fad; kad; sad; lad; ask; jad; add; dad; lad

ask a dad; ask a sad lad; all fall; fad dad salad

add salads jads all fall; all sad fad salads fall
```

Speed   The big fiend did wish for Ken to fix their giant problems.

Control   In regard to the 50th Anniversary dinner, do send our RSVP.

FaxUnlimited

112 Austin Boulevard   1-718-555-4765
Flushing, NY 11367-8875   *Fax 1-718-555-FAST*

Mach 6, 19--

Ms.
~~Mr.~~ Melody Wainwright
Elmont ~~Ag.~~ *Agency*
9852 Warren St. *sp*
New York, NY 10068

Dear Ms. Wainwrite:

It ~~is certainly~~ *was* a pleasure meeting you at our fax exhibit
at the Bentley Convention center last week. Your own
expertise and the professional level of your staff ~~was~~ *were*
really ~~outstanding.~~ *impressive.*

As I mentioned ~~to you~~ at the exhibit, our organization ~~is~~
~~in~~ need of more salespeople who know about the latest
technology. We have been turning down four out of five
potential new accounts because of the lack of qualified
salesstaff.

From our short conversation at the exhibit, I believe that
your organization is the answer. I would like to schedule
a meeting about a possible working arrangement at your
earliest convenience. *Please call to let me know what
day and time is best for you.*

Sincerely,

Linda A. Maxwell
director

rp

2 ■ *Form 17-2* ■ *Key this letter with the corrections
shown.* ■ *Find the 3 proper noun errors that Ms.
Maxwell missed.*

■ *To review Proofreaders' Marks, see page 107.*

The correct position will help you keyboard well. It will also help prevent common physical problems associated with spending hours at a keyboard. Do you remember each aspect of the correct position?

1. Position body about 8 inches from the keyboard

2. Body in line with **H** key

3. Feet on floor

4. Fingers over Home Keys

5. Wrists and back straight

6. Fingers curved to tap straight down on Home Keys

7. Wrists above keyboard (not resting on anything)

8. Eyes on copy

LESSON 2   M ■ C ■ O

Keyboard each practice line twice with single-spacing. Return twice after each two-line group.

Review

```
jj ff kk dd ll ss ;; aa jj ff kk dd ll ss ;;; aaa

jf kd ls ;a jf kd ls ;a jf kd ls ;a jf kd ls; ajf

a ja ad add jad fad lad dad sad kad all fall lass

lad; dad; kad; fad; add; lad; dad; kad; fad; add;

salk lad sal kaf ask dad salk lad sal kaf ask dad

ask dad; ask sal; ask salk; ask dad; ask sal; lad
```

FastFax Corporation
▶ 5311 Fourth Avenue   New York, NY 10017-2245 ◀

March 3, 19--

Mr. John Harvey
Bentley Convention Center
5 Market Place
Bentley, CA 90505-2849

Dear ~~Mr. Harvey!~~ *John*:

Thank you for all you cooperation in making our *equipment* exhibit ~~of fax machines~~ at the Bentley Convention Center such a success. Everone on your staff worked long and hard, and we appreciate your effort.

After ~~returning to New York~~ *I got back to the office*, I noticed that I forgot to give you the attendance reports for the sessions in which ~~Doctor~~ *Dr.* Johnston was the speaker. Since the attendance was quite good and the reports are long, I am mailing the reports rather than faxing them. You should receive them soon.

Again, John, thanks to you and *your* ~~you~~ staff for all the help. Attendence was great, and we're glad we were there.

Sincerely,

FASTFAX CORPORATION

William F. Snyder
Manger

---

1 ■ *Form 17-1* ■ *Key this letter with the corrections shown.*
■ *Find the 2 spelling errors Mr. Snyder missed.*

■ *To review Proofreaders' Marks, see page 107.*

New Reach Drill

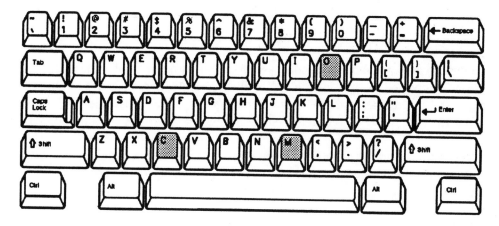

Left Hand
C ■ Use D finger

Right Hand
O ■ Use L finger
M ■ Use J finger

Watch your finger as you reach to tap each new key several times. Then make each reach without looking. With your fingers over the Home Keys, keyboard these practice lines:

```
jm jm jmj jmj mmm mmm mam mam mad mad

dd dc dcd dcd ccc ccc cac cac cad cad

lo lo lol lol ooo ooo olo olo old old
```

Accuracy Development

```
m jm jm ja ja jam jam mam mam sam sam lam lam mad

c dc dc ca ca cam cam cac cac cal cal fac fac cad

o lo lo ol ol old old sol sol jol jol fol fol lod

m jm ja c dc cad o lo old jam jam cad cad old old
```

Power Building

```
ask dad; ask sal; ask salk; ask dad; sak sal; lad

old lad sam call cad sal; ask sad dad of doll all

a sad lad looks mad; a small fad lacks mall class

jam food lacks looks class of all small fad foods

call a small food fad sad; a fad food lacks class
```

Standard report style ▪ An unbound report has left and right margins of 1 inch. If the report is to be bound on the left, increase the left margin to 1½ inches. ▪ Most reports are double-spaced. If your employer requests 3 returns rather than 4 under the title block and above a side heading, switch to single spacing and return 3 times. Then return to double-spacing. ▪ After page 1, the top margin is 1 inch.

Listing sources ▪ Some business reports contain references to other sources. Note this information in an *endnote*. Place endnotes together at the end of the report. (In WordPerfect, you can use a *footnote* just as easily. A footnote appears at the bottom of the page where the source is cited.) This style is satisfactory for most business uses:

▪ [1]Paula Theiner, <u>Northern Forests</u>, New York: Eastman Press, 1992, p. 488. *(for a book)*

▪ [1]Paula Theiner, "Fighting Acid Rain," <u>Environment Monthly</u>, pp. 103-105. *(for an article)*

To type a raised number (superscript) on a typewriter, Reverse Index once (back half a line) and type the number. Index once (ahead half a line) and type the entry. ▪ With WordPerfect, use the superscript feature or the footnote feature.

1 ▪ *Plain sheets* ▪ *Key this report.*

Monthly Report to Garden World Nurseries ▪ by Patricia McCafferty ▪ September 29, 1993 ▪ This month Hopewell Associates provided our client, Garden World Nurseries, with publicity in several areas: newspaper, trade, and radio. Account Executive Eve Wharton is also arranging for a future appearance by a Garden World Nurseries spokesperson on the very popular television show <u>Gardening with Lily</u>, hosted by Lily Richards. ¶ This month's newspaper coverage consisted of three articles mentioning Garden World Nurseries, two in the prestigious <u>The New York Times</u> gardening section and one in <u>The Daily News</u>, written by Account Executive Eve Wharton solely about Garden World Nurseries. In the first <u>New York Times</u> article,[1] columnist Joseph Elliott mentions "Garden World Nurseries of Lynbrook, Long Island, as the very best nursery for healthy bulbs. Their information staff is professional and knowledgeable; the quality of the advice about planting is first-rate, and there is courtesy all the way around." In the second article,[2] Ms. Dixon mentions Garden World's landscaping services as "one of the industry's best. The product is superb, and creativity abounds." <u>The Daily News</u> article, "Everything You Need for Fall at Garden World," by Eve Wharton,[3] was a full half-page spread on all that

Garden World offers for fall planting. ¶ This month's trade coverage consisted of a mention in the well-known trade publication, <u>Landscaping USA</u>, which mentioned Garden World's policy of guaranteeing its work for 10 years.[4] Mr. Booth also mentioned Garden World's longstanding integrity, which he said is "known throughout the industry." ¶ This month's radio coverage was on WXLI's afternoon news gardening spot, "The Green Thumb Planter." In a piece on spring bulbs, host Gerry Fields and his guest Alice Mitchell, author of <u>Gardening for Fun</u>, mentioned Garden World of Lynbrook, Long Island, as "the place to find the best bulbs outside of Holland." ▪ [1]Joseph Elliott, "Fall Planting," <u>The New York Times</u>, September 13, 1993, p. 34. ▪ [2]Christine Dixon, "Landscaping Today," <u>The New York Times</u>, September 20, 1993, p. 34. ▪ [3]Eve Wharton, "Everything You Need for Fall at Garden World," <u>The Daily News</u>, September 11, 1993, p. 26. ▪ [4]Larry Booth, "Landscaping Problems and Solutions," <u>Landscaping USA</u>, Fall 1993, p. 18.

2 ▪ *Full sheet* ▪ *Prepare a title page for the report. Use the report title, author, company name, and date given at the beginning of the report.* ▪ *Key the information centered attractively on the page.* ▪ *Try to focus attention on the report title. (See page 86, assignment 2, for an example.)*

Speed Timing

```
all sad dolls lack class; small mad mom looks sad
old food fads lack small looks of class; call dad
--1----2----3----4----5----6----7----8----9---10-
```

About Timings: You are allowed up to 4 errors. If you have 5 or more errors, the timing cannot count as an official timing test. For each error, subtract 1 word from your speed (31 words per minute with 2 errors = 29 words per minute). See *Keyboarding Essentials* for more information on timings.

How did you score? It is helpful to keep a list of daily timings. Record the date and your speed in words per minute.

LESSON 3   G ■ I ■ W

Keyboard each practice line twice with single-spacing. Return twice after each two-line group.

Review

```
ask dad; ask sal; ask salk; ask dad; ask sal; lad

old lad sam call cad sal; ask sad dad of doll all

a sad lad looks mad; a small fad lacks mall class

jam food lacks looks class of all small fad foods

call a small food fad sad; a fad food lacks class

all sad dolls lack class; small mad mom looks sad
```

L/R margins—1 inch ■ Page 1 top margin is 2 inches ■ Bottom margin—1 inch (if page number at bottom, ½" acceptable)

↓2 inches (to line 13)
RESEARCH GOALS AND SCHEDULE ↓2

by Paul Elliott ↓2

May 9, 19-- ↓4

The primary goal of this research project is to study and write about the current political status of women in Latin America. This study will involve identifying women's current status in such areas as civil rights, economic rights, and the evolving area of reproductive rights. The project staff will work with several internationally known organizations, including the Brazilian Civil Rights Coalition (BCRC), this year's sponsor of a conference on health.[1]

The project will span a year, from August through July. The research and most of the travel will take place from approximately August to April, with the remaining months devoted to writing. We will provide the University Foundation with monthly progress reports and a more detailed timetable as the project unfolds. ↓4

Resource Needs: Personnel and Budget

We realize the extent of the University Foundation's current fiscal troubles, and we appreciate its interest in funding our work. We therefore request only one full-time

1

[3-6 blank lines under number is acceptable]

New Reach Drill

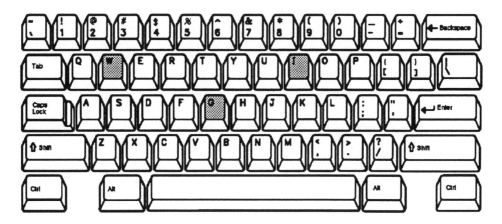

Left Hand
W ■ Use S finger
G ■ Use F finger

Right Hand
I ■ Use K finger

Watch your finger as you reach to tap each new key several times. Then make each reach without looking. With your fingers over the Home Keys, keyboard these practice lines:

```
fg fg fgf fgf ggg ggg gaf gaf gad gad

ki ki kik kik iii iii isl isl idl idl

sw sw sws sws www www wis wis wil wil
```

Accuracy Development

```
g gf gf ga ga gaf gaf gag gag jag jag lag lag sag

i ik ik is is isl isl lis lis lid lid kid kid sil

w ws ws wa wa was was law law jaw jaw saw saw wad

g gf gf i ik lik w ws was gaf gaf lid lid jag jag
```

Power Building

```
call a small food fad sad; a fad food lacks class

was sam a sad kid if dad saw a jaw gag lack class

sam was a sad old lad; if all kids saw small wigs

did old small law lack class if sam was a sad lad
```

1 ▪ *Form 15-1* ▪ *Key the letter on page 91 with the corrections you noted.* ▪ *Hand in your list of changes with the letter.*

2 ▪ *Form 15-2* ▪ *What's wrong with this table?* ▪ *Make a list of changes you would make.* ▪ *Key the table with your corrections.* ▪ *Find the 5 punctuation errors.*

GETAWAYS INTERNATIONAL
the way to travel

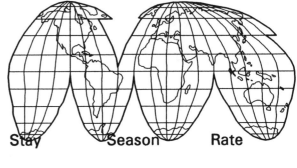

BARGAIN TRIPS

Destination	Stay	Season	Rate
Cancun, Mexico	5 days	Fall	$700
Montreal Canada	3 days	Winter	630
Tokyo, Japan	7 days	Spring	2.200
Washington, D.C.	4 days	Fall	600
New Orlean's, Louisiana	3 days	Spring	800
Castine, Maine	3 days	Fall	450
Butte, Montana	4 days	Winter	500
San Antonio, Texas	5 days	Spring	900
Great Cities, U,S.A.	11 days	Summer	2,900

Childrens' flights free with two paying adults!

Speed Timing

```
if dad was a sad lad; small food laws do lack ads
a salad jag is a small food fad of class; dad saw
--1----2----3----4----5----6----7----8----9---10-
```

LESSON 4   U ∎ E ∎ .

Keyboard each practice line twice with single-spacing. Return twice after each two-line group.

Review

```
call a small food fad sad; a fad food lacks class

was sam a sad kid if dad saw a jaw gag lack class

sam was a sad old lad; of all kids saw small wigs

did old mass laws lack class if sam was a sad lad

if dad was a sad lad; small food laws do lack ads

a salad jag is a small food fad of class; dad saw
```

New Reach Drill

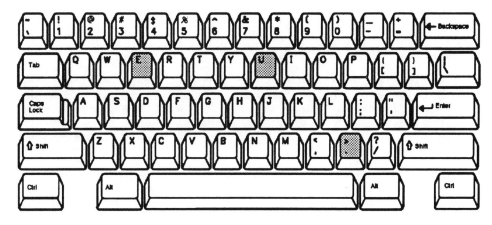

Left Hand
E ∎ Use D finger

Right Hand
U ∎ Use J finger
. ∎ Use L finger

A co-worker keyed this letter, but your employer says it is sloppy and can't be mailed. ■ *Note at least 5 changes that would improve the letter's appearance.* ■ *Find the 5 spelling errors.*

CPI

CARTWHEEL PUBLICATIONS, INC.
4907 BELMONT AVENUE
SAN FRANCISCO, CA 95416

September 13, 19--
Ms. Christie McLoud
49 Barre Street
Nashua, NH 03061

Dear Ms. McLoud:

Thank you for your order for 50 copies of *World on Wheels* and for 25 copies of our new tax guide *How to Manage Your Business*. We appreciated all the compliments you gave us regarding our service and products. I regret that some of our publications have been delayed because of a printing strike in the Bay Area. *World on Wheels* is expected in our warehouse by October 25. *How to Manage Your Business* should arrive sooner, maybe by the end of this month. These books will be shipped to you immediately upon arrival at our warehouse. The shipment is scheduled for Fourth Class delivery. If you wish, we can ship overnight through any commercial service. Shipping costs would then increase to $58.75. If you are unable to wait for these popular books, we can offer the following suggestions for possible replacements:

RACE AGAINST TIME 1991	$13.85	
BUSINESS SENSE	1989	9.95
QUICK TAX GUIDE	1990	7.99
RAY WADE'S BUSINESS GUIDE	1987	12.50
GREAT BICYCLE TRIPS	1986	15.59
GRATE BICYCLE TRIPS 2	1991	17.59
AROUND THE WORLD	1990	5.59

All these books are available now for shiping. *Race Against Time* by Jane Anders is an especially attractive book. It tells Ms. Anders' personal story of varius family trips. *Ray Wade's Business Guide* is a standard reference for people with small businesses. The book "wades" through all the technical language of the IRS publications and gives you only what you need to know.

Please call me toll-free at 1-800-555-7236 to arange for a change in your order. You can also fax a message--our number is 415-555-8273. If we don't here from you, we'll plan to ship your order immediately upon receipt of books in our warehouse. We regret the delay and will do everything we can to speed up your order.

Sincerely yours,

CARTWHEEL PUBLICATIONS, INC.

Lynn Zampieri
Customer Service

Watch your finger as you reach to tap each new key several times. Then make the reach without looking. With your eyes on the book, keyboard these practice lines:

```
ju ju juj juj uuu uuu jug jug lug lug

de de ded ded eee eee due due sue sue

l. l. l.l l.l ... ... ed. ed. el. el.
```

Accuracy Development

```
u uu uu ju ju jug jug lu lu lug lug du du dug dug

e ee ee de de dec dec se se see see le le lee lee

. .. .. l. l. el. el. d. d. ed. ed. s. s. se. se.

slug disk would look dull; doug saw dusk was due.
```

Note: Normally do not type an extra space after a period within an abbreviation (such as *U.S. history*). Type two spaces after a period at the end of a sentence.

Power Building

```
if dad was a sad lad; small food laws do lack ads

a salad jag is a small food fad of class; dad saw

dull slug disks jagged doug; would mick feed lugs

small kicks would slow fools; so will good looks.
```

Speed Timing

```
a salad jag is a small food fad of class; dad saw
mick could feed douglas food if samuel would ask.
--1----2----3----4----5----6----7----8----9---10-
```

Speed	Quantity work did make us harm the rich land for the firms.
Control	Don't write Thorne, & Sons, but please write Thorne & Sons.

Using fonts ■ The creative use of fonts can add to the effectiveness of a typed or printed document. However, too much type variety can make a document unreadable. Never use a type size that is too small for comfortable reading (unless you are keying small print!). ■ Use boldface and italics sparingly, for strong emphasis only. Too much emphasis will distract the reader.

At a typewriter ■ If a printwheel is available, switch fonts for these exercises. Use a proportional font wheel if possible. Use boldface where directed. (Be sure to switch your pitch selector to match the font.) If you don't have alternative printwheels, just use your standard font.

At a computer ■ If you are using WordPerfect, you can list available fonts on your printer by pressing Ctrl-F8 or your pull-down menu. Choose a serif font (like Times) for the letter assignment. Choose a sans serif font (like Univers) for the display assignment (exercise 2).

1 ■ *Form 14-1* ■ *Key this letter.* ■ *Use boldface for any important word, phrase, or sentence in the letter.*

Elsie Sanchez, DVM ■ Healthy Pets, Inc. ■ 16-72 Main Street ■ Tenafly, NJ 17670-4773 ■ Dear Dr. Sanchez: ■ I am the director of the Last Hope Animal Shelter. The shelter rescues, houses, and eventually finds homes for abandoned animals in the Tenafly area. In the 10 years since we began our work, the shelter has saved nearly 7,000 animals, mostly cats and dogs. However, we have also saved snakes, pigs, horses, and even two llamas from certain starvation. ¶ We are a nonprofit organization, Dr. Sanchez. We rely heavily on private grants and state funding. I don't have to tell you that with the current fiscal situation, our future is precarious at best. State funding has been cut again and again. We will survive only if people like you care enough to donate your time and expertise to our cause. Could you donate a few hours a week to examine and treat our animals? We can offer our unending appreciation as your compensation. As a member of the Tenafly community, you would encourage others to join us by helping out now. ¶ I have enclosed a table that will give you some idea of the funding situation for organizations like ours. The animals' lives are at stake. We will appreciate all the help you can give. ■ Sincerely, ■ Bob Fairchild ■ Director ■ Enclosure

2 ■ *Plain sheet, full* ■ *Arrange this table attractively. Center horizontally and vertically.* ■ *Vary fonts as desired for strong impact.* ■ *Choose a title for the table.* ■ *Check each sum in the total column for accuracy.*

Column headings ■ Year ■ Federal ■ State ■ Other ■ Total

Column 1 ■ 1989 ■ 1990 ■ 1991 ■ 1992 ■ 1993

Column 2 ■ $64,000 ■ 68,200 ■ 56,000 ■ 49,000 ■ 35,000

Column 3 ■ $34,800 ■ 27,500 ■ 22,300 ■ 23,000 ■ 19,400

Column 4 ■ $23,000 ■ 19,000 ■ 13,000 ■ 17,800 ■ 12,900

Column 5 ■ $121,800 ■ 114,700 ■ 91,300 ■ 89,800 ■ 67,300

Keyboard each practice line twice with single-spacing. Return twice after each two-line group.

Review

```
if dad was a sad lad; small food laws do lack ads

a salad jag is a small food fad of class; dad saw

dull slug disks jagged doug; would mick feed lugs

small kicks would slow fools; so will good looks.

a small food fad of class is a salad jag; saw dad

mick could feed douglas food if samuel would ask.
```

New Reach Drill

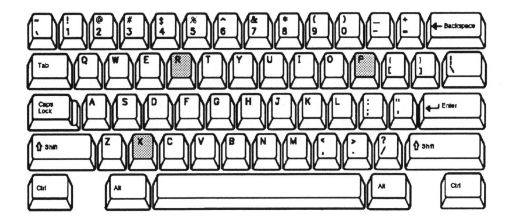

Left Hand
R ■ Use F finger
X ■ Use S finger

Right Hand
P ■ Use ; finger

Watch your finger as you reach to tap each new key several times. Make each reach without looking. Then keyboard these practice lines:

```
fr fr frf frf rrr rrr rig rig rid rid

;p ;p ;p; ;p; ppp ppp pad pad ped ped

sx sx sxs sxs xxx xxx xal xal lax lax
```

About fonts ■ A *font* is a type style. Typewriter fonts are available on printwheels. Computer and printer software offers a wide variety of fonts. Though the choice can vary greatly, type fonts have these general characteristics:

■ *Size*—Typewriter fonts are measured in pitch, characters per inch. Most typewriters offer 10-, 12-, and 15-pitch settings. Printer fonts are measured in *points*. A point is a typesetting measure. Just remember that 11-pitch type is effective for most copy. (This section is set in 11-point type.)

■ *Weight*—All fonts have varied weights. The standard weight is sometimes called *regular* (or *light* for some printer fonts). Then there is **boldface**, often used for emphasis. Some fonts have **demi** weights (extrabold). Your screen may show an *icon*, or graphic image, for boldface type.

■ *Style*—Most fonts can be set for regular (roman) or *italic* style. ***Bold italic*** is often available. Your screen may show an icon for italic type.

■ *Design*—This type is serif type. Serif type has small horizontal lines (serifs) to define the top and bottom of the letters. Sans serif type does not have serifs (see Univers below). Sans serif type is good for headings, but it is difficult to read in large blocks of type.

Font Families

Monospace type This is 12-pitch (12 cpi) Courier, a typical typewriter font. Each letter occupies the same amount of space, no matter if it is a narrow letter (like *i*) or a wide letter (like *w*). In this font, note that each letter lines up with the letter directly below. Place a ruler on the page to check. That is the easiest way to identify monospace type.

Proportional type: Univers (sans serif) In Univers, Helvetica, and other similar fonts, each letter is given space suitable to the width of the letter. For example, the *i* gets less space than the *w*. The software then moves letters closer together to avoid wide gaps. Often you can choose from among many sizes and weights (light, bold, etc.). This type is measured in *points*. This is 10-point Univers type. In general, 10-point Univers is a standard size for text. Larger sizes can be used for headings. A 17-point Univers heading looks like this:

Learning About Fonts

Proportional type: Times Roman (serif) Times Roman and other similar fonts are widely used for correspondence and reports. Like the sans serif font, this font is measured in points. This is 11-point type. Choose an 11-point Times for text copy. Count the words in a typical line of Times copy. Note how many more words can fit here, as compared with 12 cpi Courier type. Readability and space savings make this an effective font for publications.

Accuracy Development

r rr rr fr fr fre fre re re red red ro ro rod rod

p pp pp p; p; ped ped pa pa pal pal po po pod pod

x xx xx xs xs sax sax xm xm xam xam mx mx max max

rod sax was a good pal of red max; red max is lax

Power Building

a small food fad of class is a salad jag; dad saw

mick could feed douglas food if samuel would ask.

a good pal was red max; rid odd max of a red sax.

please ask douglas for a small red carriage axle.

Speed Timing

a good pal was red max; rid odd max of a red sax.
please ask douglas for a small red carriage axle.
--1----2----3----4----5----6----7----8----9---10-

LESSON 6   Y ■ Q ■ H

Keyboard each practice line twice with single-spacing. Return twice after each two-line group.

Review

a small food fad of class is a salad jag; dad saw

mick could feed douglas food if samuel would ask.

a good pal was red max; rid odd max of a red sax.

please ask douglas for a small red carriage axle.

some red carriage axles seem scarce as red disks.

losses of car sales are due; sell pals a red jag.

1 ■ *Plain sheet, full or half* ■ *Key the chart of Executive Compensation shown on page 87.* ■ *Make up at least two additional employees and their salaries and add them to the table.*

The dollar sign must align with the largest amount:

```
$  149.00
  13,335.87
```

2 ■ *Form 13-2* ■ *Key this letter. Center the table horizontally.* ■ *Leave one blank line above and below the table.*

Ms. Ann Corey ■ 14 Helena Drive ■ Wilsonville, OR 97070-4277 ■ Dear Ms. Corey ■ Thank you for sending your application and the registration check for programs this fall. We hope these seminars will prove useful to you for both the present and future. ¶ You are now registered for the following week-long seminars:

Beginning Lotus	Room A 9 a.m.
Advanced WordPerfect	Room B 1 p.m.
Publications Design	Room B 3 p.m.

These seminars will take place from Monday, April 5, through Friday, April 9. A continental breakfast is provided at our center beginning at 8 a.m. A lunch break of one hour begins at noon. For lunch, you can visit one of the many inexpensive carry-out or eat-in shops and restaurants within easy walking distance. You can also take a relaxing walk in the nearby park. ¶ I am enclosing your registration card. Please bring the card with you on Monday, April 5. If you have questions before that time, please call me. ■ Sincerely yours ■ Kylie Stevenson ■ Assistant Director ■ Enclosure

3 ■ *Plain sheet, full or half* ■ *Key this table. Center horizontally and vertically.* ■ *Note that the headings for columns 3 and 4 are longer than the items in the column. Use these headings in your key line.*

Documents for Corporate Counsel Office
March 19, 19--

CLIENT	DOCUMENT	NUMBER	FILE NAME
MacKenzie, Alfred, and Wu	Contract	5	M109.CON
Sarah Richardson	Letter	11	R39.LTR
Mason Associates	Contract	2	M21.CON
Time-Share, Inc.	Contract	23	T310.CON

New Reach Drill

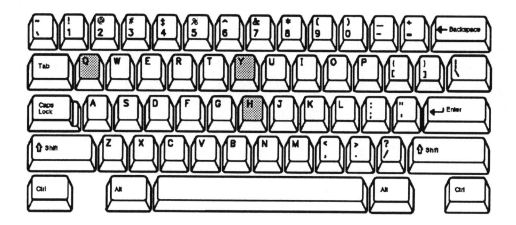

Left Hand
Q ■ Use A finger

Right Hand
Y ■ Use J finger
H ■ Use J finger

Watch your finger as you reach to tap each new key several times. Make the reaches without looking. Then keyboard these practice lines:

yj yj yjy yjy jjj jjj yyy yyy jay jay

qa qa qaq qaq juj juj eee eee que que

hj hj hjh hjh hhh hhh aaa sss has has

Accuracy Development

y yy yy yj yj yjs yjs ye ye yes yes ya ya yap yap

q qq qq qa qa qaq qaq qu qu que que qu qu qua qua

h hh hh hi hi hid hid ha ha had had he he her her

all quick rogues hide low yellow ox cars for her.

Power Building

some red carriage axles seem scarce as red disks.

losses of car sales are due; sell pals a red jag.

all quick rogues hide low yellow ox cars for her.

glossy yellow or aqua ox cars are all heard well.

Tables with money ▪ Many tables include columns that list amounts of money. To prepare a table with a column of amounts, use a *right* tab. The figures will then line up properly.

Headings over columns ▪ If the heading is wider than any item in the column, use the heading as part of the key line when you set up the table. To place headings over the columns, use the tab you already set (even if it is a right tab). Tab and keyboard the heading for each column. ▪ If you prefer the appearance of centered headings, use the space bar to visually place the headings. (This process can be time-consuming, especially if you are working with a laser printer in varied fonts.)

Tables within letters or memos ▪ For a table within a letter or memo, leave one blank line above and below the table. Center the table within the document margins. Avoid breaking a table at the bottom of the page. If you have to break the table, repeat the headings on the continuation page.

To set tabs when one column contains money amounts—

1. Clear tabs. Select your key line—the longest entry from each column. Include the dollar sign. (Example below: longest entries are *Robertson* and *$32,192.85*) The example shows 6 spaces between columns. You may want to add more space between columns for a more balanced appearance.

2. Center the key line and set a left tab for Column 1. (See Lesson 41 for review.)

3. For Column 2, note the position of the *last* character. Set a right tab or decimal tab one space after this position.

4. Clear the key line. Key the first entry in Column 1 and tab to Column 2. On a typewriter, the figures print after you press the Return Key. On a computer, figures are displayed automatically with the tab setting.

CONFIDENTIAL
Executive Compensation in 1993

Robertson	$32,192.85
Short	36,773.86
Kyte	75,033.77
Riley	99,593.71

To keyboard blocked column headings—

1. Determine the tab settings for the table as usual.

2. Tab to the first column and keyboard the heading. Repeat this process for each column.

3. Double-space or triple-space and keyboard the table.

WEST	EAST
New Mexico	Connecticut
Arizona	Rhode Island
Texas	Vermont

```
all quick rogues hide low yellow jay axes for her
sale of yellow carriage disks are as slow as aqua
--1----2----3----4----5----6----7----8----9---10-
```

LESSON 7   T ∎ N ∎ / ∎ Left Shift

Keyboard each practice line twice with single-spacing. Return twice after each two-line group.

Review

some red carriage axles seem scarce as red disks.

losses of car sales are due; sell pals a red jag.

all quick rogues hide low yellow or aqua ox cars.

yellow and aqua ox carriages are due as are axles

jill will equip yellow homes a year if she wishes

aqua houses seemed as a clue for small pool cues.

New Reach Drill

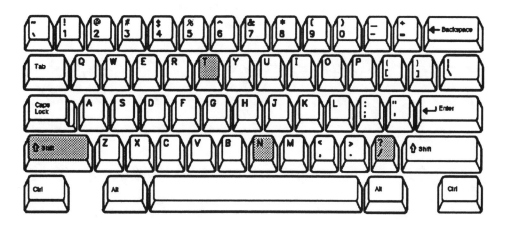

Left Hand
Left Shift ∎ Use A finger
T ∎ Use F finger

Right Hand
N ∎ Use J finger
/ ∎ Use ; finger

```
Speed      Handy pans do aid the hens to rid the lair of the fox pair.

Control    Which is pretty--Paris, France; Anchorage, Alaska; or both?
```

Automatic vertical centering ■ Many word processing programs have a vertical centering feature. You can turn on the feature before or after you key the copy to be centered. However, you should practice manual centering because typewriters do not have a vertical centering feature.

1 ■ *Plain sheet, full or half (if half, center vertically in 33 lines)* ■ *Key this list. Center each line horizontally, and center the list vertically on the page.* ■ *Double-space after the heading.*

FEATURED TOPICS

American Constitutional Law
The Federal Courts
Constitutional Thought and Theory
The Supreme Court This Century

2 ■ *Plain sheet, full or half.* ■ *Key the table shown on page 85. Center the table vertically and horizontally.*

3 ■ *Plain full sheet* ■ *Center this report cover sheet vertically and horizontally.* ■ *Double-space after the first line. Return 4 to 6 times before the writer's name and before the date.* ■ *Save the document for reference later.*

Recycling Solutions for Tomorrow:

A Report to the Urban Planning Council

by Thomas C. Miller
Senior Analyst
Wark Brothers, Inc.

January 19, 19--

4 ■ *Plain half sheet* ■ *Center this notice vertically and horizontally. You should have 2 lines of copy before the list.* ■ *Return 3 times (2 blank lines) before the table.* ■ *Double-space the table.*

Please check the list below for your course days and location. If you have a scheduling conflict, see Mrs. Blymun in Room 215.

Keyboarding	MWF	265 Holt Hall
Accounting	M	Auditorium
Computer Applications	TTh	400 Kiley Building
Business English	MWF	105 Holt Hall
Computer Lab	W	2 B Building

Practice each new reach, and then type the practice lines. To type a capital letter with the right hand: Hold down the **Left Shift** Key and type the letter. Space twice after a period.

```
tf tf tft tft fff iii ttt ttt fit fit

nj nj njn njn nnn sss iii nnn sin sin

I saw Jill.  Let me go.  Kay was ill.

/; /; /; /;/; a/an; a/an; and/or and/
```

Accuracy Development

```
t tt tt ft ft fit fit st st sit sit lt lt lit lit

n nn nn jn jn jan jan dn dn dan dan fn fn fan fan

I saw the formats of the program.  Len stored it.

Keep Len and/or Janet informed of his/her format.
```

Power Building

```
Jill will equip yellow homes a year if she wants.

aqua houses seemed as a clue for small pool cues.

Len and/or Jan kept me informed about the matter.

Keep the ax clue for his/her file.  Lift the tag.
```

Speed Timing

```
Lift the tag and hold for Jan.  His/her report is
due on Monday.  I will tell Ken and/or Mary then.
--1----2----3----4----5----6----7----8----9---10-
```

↓66 lines on a full-size sheet (8½ x 11")

To *manually* center copy vertically—

1. Count the lines of type in your copy. (Example below: 7 lines of type)

2. Count the blank lines in your copy. (Example below: 6 blank lines)

3. Add the lines of copy and the blank lines. (Example below: 13 lines)

4. Subtract the total lines in copy from the total lines on page (66 − 13 = 53)

5. Divide the result by 2. (The answer tells you how many blank lines to leave above and below your copy.) If you get a fraction, give the extra line to the top. (53 ÷ 2 = 26½. Therefore, the top margin has 27 lines and the bottom margin has 26 lines; total 53.)

↓27 blank lines (28 returns)

1 (This is line 28)	INSTRUCTOR LIST		
2	Spring Semester ↓3		
3			
4			
5	Keyboarding	Weidman	X1900
6			
7	Accounting	Gleason	X3425
8			
9	Computer Applications	Okin	X2640
10			
11	Business English	McLaughlin	X4002
12			
13	Computer Lab	Carbone	X2350

↓26 blank lines to bottom

Keyboard each practice line or group of lines twice with single-spacing. Return twice after each group.

Review

Jill will equip yellow homes a year if she wants.

aqua houses seemed as a clue for small pool cues.

Len and/or Jan kept me informed about the matter.

Keep the ax clue for his/her file. Lift the tag.

Lift the tag and hold for Jan. His/her report is due on Monday. I will tell Ken and/or Mary then.

New Reach Drill

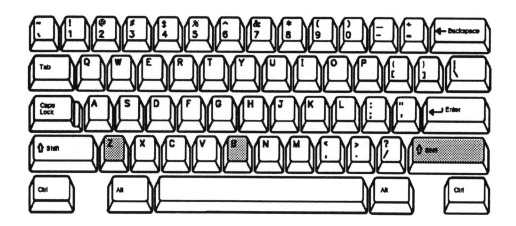

Left Hand
B ■ Use F finger
Z ■ Use A finger

Right Hand
Right Shift ■ Use ; finger

Practice making each new reach several times. To type a capital with the left hand: Hold down the **Right Shift** key and type the letter. Then keyboard these practice lines:

bf bf bfb bfb fff iii bbb bbb fib fib

Dad saw Doreen. Take Test A Tuesday.

za za zaz zaz jjj aaa zzz jaz jaz zap

```
Speed      The big city firms' "vow" is to make the handy dock for us.

Control    Please use Line 47 soon to call 1-800-555-3782 for No. 18s.
```

Automatic centering ■ As you can see, manual centering of lines can involve tedious counting. When a typist is backspacing to center a line, just one small distraction can mean starting all over. Therefore, automatic centering is a standard feature for all electronic typewriters and for word processing software. Just remember that the automatic feature isn't performing any mysterious tricks—it is just doing the manual steps for you.

On a typewriter ■ Be sure you have set the right margin, and then—

■ Move to the center point.

■ Backspace once for every two characters in the key line.

■ Type the key line. Set a tab for each column.

On a computer ■ In WordPerfect, use the steps listed above or use the center function (Shift-F6). Then type the word or the table key line and press Enter to turn off centering. For columns, note the horizontal position of each column on the lower right of the screen. Set an absolute tab for each column. *To set tabs, also see **Relative tabs**.*

Relative tabs ■ If you set *relative* tabs in WordPerfect, note that the 0 point on the tab scale is the left margin, not the edge of the paper. When you note the tab settings from the screen, subtract the left margin width to get the correct tab indent from the margin. (Check your manual.)

Margins ■ With electronic equipment, the center point is the midpoint between the left and right margins. If your copy does not look centered, check to be sure you set a right margin.

1 ■ *Plain sheet, half or full* ■ *Key this centered list. Underline the headings as shown. Double-space between groups.*

COMMITTEE ASSIGNMENTS

Personnel & Budget Committee
Susan Powers
Blanche Lim
James Lynch

Resources Committee
Lila Weiner
Charles Gibbons
Mona Tzadwecheck
Roy Lightfoot

2 ■ *Plain sheet, half or full* ■ *Key the two-column table shown in the lower box on page 83.*

Center the heading. Double-space. Then type the table. Tab from the first column to the second. (Do not use the Space Bar.)

Note on Space Bar ■ On a computer, never use the space bar to insert extra space. Use tabs. Then you can avoid uneven spacing if you use a laser printer with varied fonts (Lesson 44 offers more information on laser fonts).

b bb bb bf bf fib fib bi bi bib bib li li lib lib

Daniel saw Stacey with the computer program disk.

Sal got zapped with some more of the static jazz.

The blank disk should initialize count with zero.

Power Building

Keep the ax clue for his/her file. Lift the tab.

The computer disk program should begin with zero.

Some systems may crash due to static electricity.

Let him/her take the boxes of cardboard to Wally.

Speed Timing

Bill bids to initialize the computer program disk
with zero. Lost static electricity made a crash.
--1----2----3----4----5----6----7----8----9---10-

LESSON 9   , ■ V ■ ?

Keyboard each practice line or group of lines twice with single-spacing. Return
twice after each group.

Review

Keep the ax clue for his/her file. Lift the tab.

Lift the tab and hold for Jan. His/her report is
due on Monday. I will tell Ken and/or Mary then.

Wally took cartons of cardboard to reprographics.

Bill bids to initialize the computer program disk
with zero. Lost static electricity made a crash.

←a full-size sheet measures 85 spaces across in 10-pitch type (102 in 12-pitch)→

To *manually* center a word or line of type—

1. Clear tabs.

2. Count the characters in the line to be centered. Include spaces. (Example below: 20)

3. Tab or move to center. (42 for 10-pitch; 51 for 12-pitch)

4. Backspace once for every 2 characters. (Example below: backspace 10 times)

5. Type the line.

12345678901234567890
PACKING REQUIREMENTS

←a full-size sheet measures 85 spaces across in 10-pitch type (102 in 12-pitch)→

To *manually* center separate groups of words (columns), use a key line—

1. Clear tabs.

2. Determine your key line. Count the spaces in the longest word in each column. (Example below: Ellen Rodriguez = 15 and Word Processing Specialist = 26) Add 6 spaces for the space between columns. (Example below: add 6 spaces—total 47) Total spaces in key line = 47.

4. Tab or move to center. (42 for 10-pitch; 51 for 12-pitch)

5. Backspace once for every 2 characters. (Example below: backspace 23 times)

6. Set a tab where Column 1 begins.

7. Type the longest entry in Column 1, plus 6 spaces for the space between columns. (Example total = 20) Set a tab at this position. This is where Column 2 begins.

8. Delete the key line (keep tab settings) or get a clean piece of paper.

OFFICE DIRECTORY

```
        Kathy Abudazzi        Manager
        Alice Abrams          Word Processing Specialist
        Jim Boskey            Systems Analyst
        Carl Clark            Administrative Secretary
        Ellen Rodriguez       Technical Support
        Bill Travers          Computer Operator
        Sally Williams        Supervisor
```

New Reach Drill

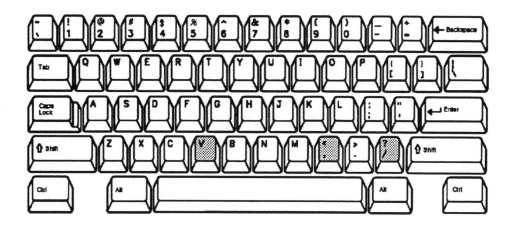

Left Hand
V ■ Use F finger

Right Hand
, ■ Use K finger
? ■ Use ; finger

Practice each new reach several times, and then keyboard these practice lines:

,k ,k ,k, ,k, kkk ,,, ad, ad, al, al,

vf vf vfv vfv fff vvv aaa fav fab val

Is Ben here? Were disks seen by Kip?

Note: Type one space after a comma (,) within a sentence. Type two spaces after a question mark (?) at the end of a sentence.

Accuracy Development

, ,, ,, k, k, ,k, ,k, d, d, ad, ad, l, l, al, al,

v vv vv vf vf vfv vfv av av fav fav vl vl val val

Will he go? Is the tube here? What about disks?

If the valve is closed, the flavor control can no longer operate. Should Mr. Clar close the valve?

Format errors include incorrect spacing and a ragged right margin. They also include incorrect punctuation and elements shown out of order.

■ **Find the 10 format errors in this letter. Use Example 1 (page 62) as a guide.**

QUALITY CARPET, INC.
40 Broadway
Pittsburgh, PA 15132-1522

July 12, 19--

Ms. Dolores Delgado
Crescent Mills
Ellington, NJ 07801-2170
Corporate Plaza

Dear Ms. Delgado

Thank you for taking so much time this morning to assist
me with this order. As I explained, my client wants a
full wool weave, which is not easy to find anymore.
Synthetic weaves are of high
quality and can be produced more cheaply.

     I am interested in seeing samples of both lines of
wool carpet that Crescent Mills produces. I will call
you as soon as possible with a purchase selection. I
expect to make my choice by next Wednesday.

                         Sincerely
                         QUALITY CARPET, INC.

Cynthia Wiker,
Vice President
ss

Power Building

Lost static electricity caused the word system to
crash. When Bob arrives, have him do me a favor.

Is he here yet? If so, send him to the data file
to obtain either/or information on center valves.

Steven backed up the hard disk section on several
floppies. Will your arrangement be satisfactory?

If so, please send the reprographic statistics to
Two Central for appropriate processing by Monday.

Speed Timing

The new flavor control valve data has not arrived
as planned. Shall we call about the development?
--1----2----3----4----5----6----7----8----9---10-

LESSON 10   Basic Keyboard Review

You are now familiar with the alphabetic keys on your keyboard! In this lesson,
you review the alphabetic keys.

Keyboard each practice line or group of lines twice with single-spacing. Return
twice after each group.

Review

awake bike color drake edge fort grape harm input

jolly kick legal memo note other party quip refer

sale time usual vogue wait xenia young zest media

Input the grape color to refer to the other part.

Note legal memos that quip usual media sale time.

Proofreading memos ■ Memos are normally sent to another person within the same company. They serve as a permanent record of company communications. Proofread memos with the same attention you give to letters sent to people outside the company.

Paper size ■ A memo may be printed on a half sheet (8½ by 5½") or on a full sheet (8½ by 11"). Examples 5 and 6 are shown on half sheets.

Margins ■ Use standard margin settings of 1 inch for most memos (a 6½" line).

1 ■ *Form 9-1* ■ *Keyboard Example 5.*

2 ■ *Plain paper, half or full sheet* ■ *Key Example 6.*

3 ■ *Form 9-3* ■ *Key this memo. Use the standard memo format (Example 5).*

TO: Leslie Kahn, Supervising Attorney ■ FROM: Brian Marsh, Staff Attorney ■ DATE: August 9, 19-- ■ SUBJECT: Client Interview ■
I interviewed Maria Ramos this afternoon. She is still very upset about losing her job and is not ready to decide at this time about her course of action. However, I think she will eventually decide to sue her employer, Martindale Boating, for wrongful discharge. ¶ Since Martindale has a written company policy guaranteeing maternity leave, I believe Ms. Ramos has a strong case.

4 ■ *Form 9-4* ■ *Key this memo in simplified format (Example 6).*

Brian Marsh, Staff Attorney ■ August 19, 19-- ■ POSSIBLE RAMOS SUIT ■ I have looked over the Maria Ramos file, and I agree that her case is strong. You have thoroughly checked the facts and circumstances. The details of Martindale Boating's actions are in our favor, and you can make that clear in any possible suit. ¶ Please let me know which Martindale employees you plan to call as witnesses and report on your interviews with them. Leslie Kahn ■ Supervising Attorney

5 ■ *Form 9-5* ■ *Key this memo in standard format.*

TO: All Support Staff ■ FROM: Director of Human Services ■ DATE: June 1, 19-- ■ SUBJECT: Summer Hours ■ Because our experiment with a shortened work week was such a success last year, we will be implementing the schedule again this year. ¶ Beginning the third week in June, all support staff will begin work at 8 a.m. and leave work at 5:30 p.m. A half-hour lunch break will be allowed. This schedule will enable you to have Fridays off. ¶ Enjoy!

6 ■ *Form 9-6* ■ *Use simplified format for this memo.*

Steven Lock ■ November 4, 19-- ■ WILSON INVESTIGATION ■ I parked outside Richard Wilson's house this morning at around 4 a.m. At 7 a.m., Mr. Wilson left his house and drove approximately 12 miles to a parking garage construction site. He worked at this location lifting heavy materials and climbing ladders until 3:30 p.m. ¶ Based on the day's observations, it does not seem likely that Mr. Wilson has a back problem. I never saw him take an extra break, and he climbed into his car easily to drive home. ■ Meg Sumner ■ Investigator

Control Development

The tables for the report are not in proper form.
Pam believes that our computer is capable of some
very complex tasks. We should include the yearly
budget projections when we design spreadsheets or
use old ones to decrease our workload this April.

Accuracy Development

The basic keyboard has a main role in information
processing systems. In fact, the inventor of the
first typewriter wanted to overcome large expense
associated with preparing documents in a way that
was quicker than carving any wood printing plate.

Power Building

Keyboard the paragraphs in 2 minutes, if possible. If you complete both
paragraphs within this time, begin again.

Normally, a space follows a comma when it appears
in a sentence; one space comes after a semicolon;
two spaces then follow a period after a sentence.
Dr. and Mrs. are courtesy title abbreviations and
are followed by only one space after that period.

In numerical copy, punctuation is sometimes typed
differently from punctuation in typewritten text.
Also, the colon has many applications that may be
important if you are keyboarding any numerical or
statistical copy. These uses will be shown soon.

Control Timing

Keyboard the following paragraph and fill in the missing words as you type. If
you complete the paragraph within the time allotted, begin the paragraph again.


```
A comma is normally followed by ___ space when it  [one]
is used in a sentence.  ___ spaces follow periods  [Two]
at the ends of sentences, and ___ space must come  [one]
after a period at the ___ of abbreviations.  Then  [end]
a semicolon should be followed by only ___ space.  [one]
--1----2----3----4----5----6----7----8----9---10-
```

Memorandum

↓up to 1 inch (6 lines) under printed heading
TO: David Chang, Editor ↓2   ←set tab for heading information

FROM: Reginald Goldwater, President ↓2

DATE: October 19, 19-- ↓2

SUBJECT: Old World Collectibles Catalog Errors ↓3

Please check the galleys of this month's catalog for price
errors in the Rare Books category. Our $5100.30 Henry
James manuscript is listed for $510.03, and on the same
page the Jane Austen letter is incorrectly listed at $7.00
rather than $700.00. ↓2

Last month's catalog went to press with errors. I hope
you can find the source of these problems. ↓2

gp

Example 5
Standard Memo Format

↓2 inches (13 lines) if no printed heading
Reginald Goldwater ↓2

October 20, 1992 ↓2

OLD WORLD COLLECTIBLES ERRORS ↓3   ←use all caps

Thank you for pointing out the errors in this month's
catalog. We had discovered them earlier in the day, and
we have faxed the corrections to the typesetter. We
expect corrected copy within 24 hours. I'll be sure you
see the corrected pages before we proceed. ↓2

I regret these mistakes. I should have a list of possible
new typesetters within a week. ↓3

Dave Chang, Editor ↓2

rt

Example 6
Simplified Memo Format

Keyboarding numbers by touch may seem difficult at first, but with practice you will soon keyboard numbers easily.

Keyboard each practice line twice with single-spacing. Return twice after each group.

Review

jad; dad; kad; fad; add; lad; gad; had; sad; lads

add a flask; add half glass flasks; a flask falls

Please do wipe the yellow taxi windows carefully.

Harsh sales memos resulted from our legal quakes.

The vat color media is fixed by zebra references.

New Reach Drill

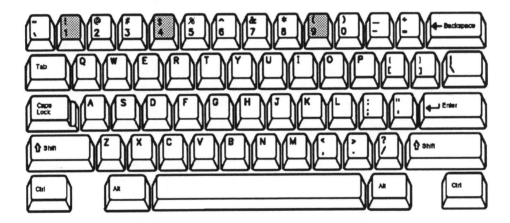

Left Hand
1 ■ Use A finger
4 ■ Use F finger

Right Hand
9 ■ Use L finger

Practice each new reach several times. With your fingers over the Home Keys, keyboard these practice lines. (Line 1, type 1 (one) key. Line 2, letter *l*.)

a aa aaa aq a aql 1 11 111 a1a 111 1a1

1 11 111 1 19 9 99 999 191 919 999 111

f ff fff f f4 4 44 444 f4f 4f4 444 f44

```
Speed      Aid the sick auditor with work to fix their title problems.

Control    The meeting rooms will accommodate eighteen to fifty-three.
```

Zip code placement ■ Leave at least 1 space before the zip code. The illustrations and exercises in this text show 2 spaces before the zip code. This spacing is preferred by the U.S. Postal Service. However, 1 space is acceptable.

Full zip code ■ Use the 9-digit zip code whenever available. In the future, mail discounts will apply to mail with the correct scannable format (all caps, no punctuation, suitable abbreviations, full zip).

WordPerfect users and other software users ■ You can create a *style*, *macro*, or *file* to make envelope preparation easier. A WordPerfect envelope format is available in the page format menu (Shift-F8, Paper Size/Type), or use the pull-down menu.

Folding letters for envelope insertion ■ See page 103 for folding instructions.

1 ■ *Forms 8-1 through 8-5* ■ *Prepare a No. 10 envelope for each address. Use either the standard format or the all-caps format.*

Abbreviations ■ These common words are abbreviated in the all-caps format:

AVENUE	AVE
BOULEVARD	BLVD
DRIVE	DR
LANE	LN
ROAD	RD
STREET	ST

Always use the two-letter state abbreviation. This list is provided on page 103.

Ms. Emily Crawley ■ Sumner Industries ■ 50 Carl Lane ■ Westbury, NY 11590-2236

Mr. George Foley ■ Marshall Associates ■ 16 Treflin Road ■ St. Paul, MN 55164-0422

Mr. Joseph Demira ■ Global Services ■ 34-23 88th Street ■ Redding, CT 06896-2256

Ms. Gemma Riley ■ Epic Flooring ■ 72 Main Street ■ Terre Haute, IN 47811-9972

Ms. Anna Perez ■ Compu Chip Industries ■ 14 Sunrise Boulevard ■ Monroe, MI 48161-2258

2 ■ *Forms 8-6 through 8-10* ■ *Prepare a No. 6¾ envelope for each address below. Use the all-caps address style (use the abbreviations given in column 1 on this page).*

Dr. Sam Chin
Ashton Technologies
88 Ross Road
Portland, OR 97205-9076

Ms. Rita Silverman
Whitecap Labs
Corporation Drive
Paradise, CA 95969-7421

Ms. Norma Parades
Community Hospital
700 Richmand Road
Syracuse, NY 13210-8833

Oscar Blake, Esquire
Tulsa Legal Services
945 Deep Pond Avenue
Tulsa, OK 74102-2946

Ms. Marie LaRue
Upton Laboratories
6609 Collier Drive
Montreat, NC 28757-0876

Accuracy Development

There were 191 bytes left on hard disk number 91.

Please return data pack 44 to 494 Rabling Street.

Did the report indicate 41, 44, or 49 disks lost?

Inventory records reflect 94 valves or 149 plugs.

Power Building

If the report indicated that 91 people are in the audience survey, then the summary would reflect a change of 41 percent. This change will cause the engineer to adjust the applause regulator to 491. A sound disturbance level of 491 is satisfactory.

Of the 94 students enrolled in the 19 information processing classes, 49 will receive instructional activities on Model 119 computerized transcribing equipment in the reprographics center. Has Laura completed Lesson 4 on the Model 11? Let me know.

Speed Timing

Laura completed Lesson 19 and proceeded to obtain the necessary information for sending the 94 boys to camps. The number of boys who applied for all jobs this year did decrease by 41 percent, making this task complicated since 914 vacancies opened.
--1----2----3----4----5----6----7----8----9---10-

STROUD ENGINEERING COMPANY
109 Hargett Lane
Jacksonville, FL 32219-1002

↓2.5 inches

indent 4 inches—set tab→

Ms. Ann Corey
Sound Systems, Inc.
4901 Maidenchoice Lane
Newark, DE 19715-9983

[bottom margin at least 5/8 inch; right margin of at least 1 inch]

No. 10 envelope with company return address (9½ by 4⅛ inches)

indent ½ inch→

↓½ inch
Florence Mendoza
47 Hanai Way
Honolulu, HI 96822

↓2 inches

indent 2½ inches—set tab→

MR GREG M TYLER
CAREER TRAINING CORPORATION
1654 KAPIOLANI BLVD
HONOLULU HI 96814-7362

[bottom margin at least 5/8 inch; right margin at least 1 inch]

No. 6¾ envelope with typed return address (6½ by 3⅝ inches)

Address style for automated processing ■ The U.S. Postal Service (USPS) recommends the use of all-caps lettering with no punctuation. The lower envelope above meets USPS standards for automated processing. For first-class mail, both addressing styles shown above are acceptable.

Keyboard each practice line twice with single-spacing. Return twice after each two-line group.

Review

Did my report indicate 11 or 111 bytes remaining?

There are 999 students enrolled in the 99 events.

How many of the 444 participants are in Event 44?

The 19 students did score 49 on 194 items tested.

Experiment 41 shows a variance between 14 and 91.

New Reach Drill

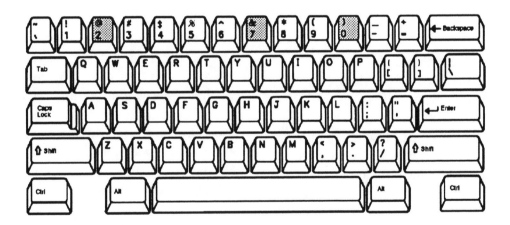

Left Hand
2 ■ Use S finger

Right Hand
7 ■ Use J finger
0 ■ Use ; finger

Practice each new reach several times. Then keyboard these practice lines:

```
; ;; ;;; ;p; ; ;p0 0 00 000 ;0; 000 0;0

s ss sss sws s sw2 2 22 222 s2s 222 2s2

j jj jjj juj j ju7 7 77 777 j7j 777 7j7
```

```
Speed     Nan did work to rush giant pens with soap for the neighbor.

Control   Send the new travel planners to Ms. McLaughlin in Syracuse.
```

Full return address ■ When you send a personal business letter, be sure to include your complete return address. At times you may want to include your work or home telephone number in the address block at the top of the page.

Varying placement ■ For a short letter, begin the return address 2 or 3 inches from the top of the page. For a long letter, begin the return address 1 or 2 inches from the top.

Alternate format ■ If you prefer, you can start with the date in the normal position (2.5 inches from the top). Then place your return address directly under your name in the signature block.

1 ■ *Plain sheet* ■ *Keyboard Example 4.*

Keyboard the example as shown. Use the default margins on your word processing software (normally 1-inch margins).

Date ■ Use today's date.

2 ■ *Plain sheet* ■ *Keyboard this letter in the alternate format described above. This letter is of average length.*

386 Central Avenue ■ Southside, IA 51250-2234 ■ Mr. Jake Wilson, President ■ STAR Sports Equipment ■ 2 Bell Boulevard ■ Crofton, OK 74820-3356 ■ Dear Mr. Wilson: ■ This box contains the STAR Sports deluxe football helmet I bought for my son only a week ago. As you can see, there is a deep dent on the left side of the helmet. This damage occurred during a routine play at a practice session. This is the third helmet he has used, and both of the others lasted much longer than one week. ¶ I am concerned about the flimsy quality of this helmet. I am especially concerned because this helmet exposed my son to serious head injuries. Luckily he received only a bruise this time. Next time he might not be so lucky. ¶ I purchased your deluxe model because it claims to be the best protection available for children. My son was not protected. I don't know if you have had other complaints about the helmet, but even one injury is too many. I hope you will test the helmet's safety and not hesitate to make needed changes.

¶ I am requesting a full refund for this product. The enclosed receipt will verify the purchase date. I feel certain you will find this demand reasonable, considering the circumstances. ■ Sincerely, ■ Margery Lot

3 ■ *Plain sheet* ■ *Keyboard this letter, using Example 4 as a format guide.*

183 South 92nd Street ■ Silver Pond, MI 49201-1777 ■ Mr. Robert Acevado, Vice President ■ Orange Bus Line ■ 6 Port Road ■ Ann Arbor, MI 49319-0087 ■ Dear Mr. Acevado: ■ I am writing to let you know that the quality of service on the Orange Bus Line is deteriorating. I have used Orange Line buses for more than 20 years, and I have always been satisfied with the service. On the whole, buses have been on schedule, coming every 15 minutes. ¶ Today, however, I waited 45 minutes for a bus. It was <u>very</u> cold outside today, Mr. Acevado. Lately I have found that this is not an unusual amount of time to wait for an Orange Line bus. The other day I waited 50 minutes and then took a cab. Like many other people, I cannot afford cabs. ¶ Please look into this matter. I do not want to have to find another way to get to work, but if your service continues as it is, I will have no choice. Thank you for your attention. ■ Sincerely, ■ Jay Flynn

Accuracy Development

Prefix the basic data program with 0 on item 004.

The 222 members of the staff won 22 big trophies.

Production for Vat 777 accelerated to 77 percent.

The budget account number for Personnel is 0.702.

Power Building

The equipment reports reveal 40 errors associated
with a static reading of over 72. An article may
indicate that if static readings go over 70, some
immediate attention could be given by adjusting a
red control knob stamped with the number 0.270.S.

Kindly forward Budget Report 94 to 427 Washington
Way, Pittsburgh, Pennsylvania 14079, by Thursday.
If there is no reply to our June 10 memo, respond
in a positive manner to the Rand 900 Corporation,
1904 Association Boulevard, Omni, Illinois 42710.

Speed Timing

At least 27 of the 94 applicants will not qualify
for the 71 positions available in our 4 stores in
the Eastern Region. Could I request that Store 1
reduce to 11 the number of critical new positions
required for their operation in central Virginia?
--1----2----3----4----5----6----7----8----9---10-

↓1 to 3 inches

519 Walnut Lane
Stroudsburg, PA   18301-4312
April 12, 19--↓4

Ms. Fiona McDonough
Irish Tourist Board
Comstock Plaza
Chicago, IL   30333-2214 ↓2

Dear Ms. McDonough: ↓2   ←mixed punctuation used more often than open

I noticed the Irish Tourist Board's advertisement in the
Stroudsburg Gazette today and would like to receive the free
booklet you mention about trips to Ireland. I am especially
interested in County Galway and would appreciate information
about places to stay in Galway City.

I am planning to travel with my two young daughters. Please
include any information you may have about places of interest
to children. We expect to travel in the summer.

Thank you for providing these materials.

Sincerely, ↓4

Mary McTaggart
Mary McTaggart

Example 4
Personal Business Letter
Mixed Punctuation

Keyboard each practice line twice with single-spacing. Return twice after each two-line group.

Review

Did 27 of the 94 applicants qualify for the task?

Of the 71 positions available, 40 are in Florida.

Account 0.42791 indicated shortage on line .0017.

Critical limits 11 and 9 were reached on Tuesday.

March awards boasted 270 honors in 49 categories.

New Reach Drill

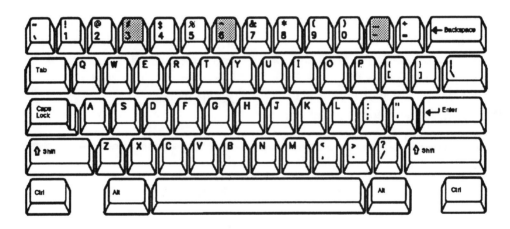

Left Hand
3 ■ Use D finger

Right Hand
6 ■ Use J finger
- ■ Use ; finger

Practice each new reach several times. Then keyboard these practice lines:

; ;; ;;; ;p; ; p;- - -- --- ;-; --- -;-

d dd ddd ded d de3 3 33 333 d3d 333 3d3

j jj jjj jyj j jy6 6 66 666 j6j 666 6j6

2 ■ *Form 6-2* ■ *Keyboard this letter using the modified block format (Example 2) with mixed punctuation.*

Mr. Ricardo Espinoza ■ New Start Computer Corporation ■ 2128 Satellite Drive ■ Baltimore, MD 21217-5891 ■ Dear Mr. Espinoza: ■ We have now had a month to sample the computer software system your company provided Blue Hook. We are all very impressed with the New Start quality, and we look forward to learning more about the system capabilities. However, we do have a few suggestions for improvements in our customized version. ¶ Though the software has enhanced our capabilities in several areas, we have a few problems with certain features. For example, it is still too easy to lose documents. The other day one of our advertising executives lost all the graphics for a Swiss Watch campaign she had spent weeks developing. She lost marketing, demographic and field research charts that were essential to our advertising strategy. The Swiss Watch people were dissatisfied with our services, and the delay could have cost more than our embarrassment. A representative from your company was able to retrieve the information, but hours were lost--hours we can't afford. We need a system that backs up documents much more easily and thoroughly than this. ¶ Another problem is the amount of time it takes to find documents. Blue Hook Advertising has over 100 clients. We input thousands of documents a year. We need a clear, easily maintained filing system. We do not need a system that slowly searches every document by order of entry. If I am looking for the Viva Cream Account, I do not want to wait through A-U. I hope you can adjust this feature. ¶ Finally, we would like access to more colors. The blue and green print very nicely, but the purple looks black and the red is too pale. We need vivid colors. Color is a big part of advertising. We have meetings about colors, and the ones we are printing out with the New Start System have to be better. I have enclosed a paint chart from our ink supplier; the colors we need are circled. ¶ I am interested in developing these custom features to use your system to its fullest here at Blue Hook. I look forward to our network training session next week--I know we will all learn a lot from your trainers. We have set aside a room with a projector and a conference table for the seminar. Please have your trainers plan to have lunch with our staff that day. ¶ You can call me directly on my private line to discuss these matters at your convenience. ■ Sincerely ■ Henry Ditworth ■ President ■ Enclosure

200+ words

Two-Page Letter Pointers

Two-page letters are relatively time-consuming. You can prepare one-page letters much more quickly.

If you are preparing a letter that runs over to a second page, determine whether you can make the letter take up only one page instead. Consider the following:

■ Decreasing margins ■ Changing font to a smaller size (10 cpi to 12 cpi)

Don't make the page look too full if you make these adjustments. If you have to prepare a two-page letter, be sure the plain second sheet matches the letterhead in color and weight. Many offices buy special paper for this purpose.

Accuracy Development

Part-time employment works with long-range plans.

Are you sure my number is 036-33-6036? Check it.

Leave the 33 shirts and 6 jackets at the laundry.

There are 63 up-to-date examples of hyphen usage.

Power Building

The tax-exempt securities represented one-half of
the investment package offered by four long-range
plans presented at my conference. Please consult
page 9 in the low-risk directory and indicate the
first, second, and third choices on the red form.

After checking the number 036-33-6036, I find the
number to be in error. This number is now eliminated from the January 19 report, and the revised
number, 207-19-0497, is included on my February 4
report. I hope this last-minute change is right.

Speed Timing

Number 24 has been eliminated from the on-the-job
training package for office staff in our Lawrence
office. Shall we consider 63 as a substitute kit
for this term, and/or would 179 serve our purpose
more adequately? Please send first-hand comment.
--1----2----3----4----5----6----7----8----9---10-

LESSON 14   8 ■ 5 ■ =

Keyboard each practice line twice with single-spacing. Return twice after each
two-line group.

Review

Here are the 240 items that were in her order 63.

Consider 27 responses as representing two-thirds.

Just place his/her payroll data in Account 0.903.

Will my 126 tax-exempt contributions be deducted?

I can be called after 2 p.m. at 796-0371 or 0372.

```
Speed      The big jay did aid them when he held us idle with the pal.

Control    Debbie saw three odd trees falling near the bubbling brook.
```

Italics ■ If you are working at a typewriter, use the underline feature as shown in the assignments below. If you are working at a computer, use *italics* (slanted type) wherever you see underlined text.

Bottom margin ■ Don't try to fit too much copy onto page 1 of your two-page letter. At a typewriter, make a light pencil mark 1½ inches from the bottom edge of the page. When you see this mark while typing, make your page-ending decision. (Later erase the mark.) On a computer, note where the program breaks the page as you keyboard. Your program is probably set for a 1-inch bottom margin. This page break is acceptable for your two-page letter.

Acceptable paragraph break at bottom ■ Avoid widows and orphans (a single line of a paragraph at the bottom or top of a page). Your word processing software may have a feature that prevents widows and orphans when a page break is inserted. Sometimes you can add space above the date line (move the entire letter down one or more lines) to make an acceptable page break. Don't leave only the signature block on page 2 of a letter, and avoid hyphenating the last word on the page.

1 ■ *Form 6-1* ■ *Key this two-page letter in full block format (Example 1) with open punctuation.*

Ms. Emily Jackson ■ Garden World Nurseries ■ 17 Bluebell Crescent ■ Lynbrook, NY 11582-3907 ■ Dear Ms. Jackson ■ Hopewell Associates is a mid-size horticultural public relations firm that provides horticultural suppliers and large nurseries, like Garden World Nurseries, with the media exposure your business deserves. In today's highly competitive marketplace, our services can make the difference between merely surviving and thriving. With a young, energetic, and award-winning staff, Hopewell Associates can make your business even more successful. We are not another advertising agency. Hopewell takes off where your advertising stops by providing your business with extensive newspaper, trade, radio, and television coverage. With a Hopewell publicity campaign, Garden World Nurseries will be the only world for all nursery needs. ¶ We have enclosed an outline for a possible publicity campaign for Garden World Nurseries. As you will notice, we take a seasonal approach to the campaign, stressing your company's particular outstanding offers for each time of the year. You would be surprised how many potential customers never think of nurseries while planning their Christmas festivities. With a Hopewell campaign, they will realize that there's more than Christmas trees to buy at Garden World Nurseries. While the children visit Santa at Garden World, their parents can shop for that last-minute gift or those needed Christmas ornaments. Believe us, your sales will make for a very happy holiday. ¶ Your busy time of the year will also be even busier with Hopewell working for you. We envision a Fall Planting campaign, with a Garden World Nurseries spokesperson appearing on local radio programs to give listeners (and consumers) tips on fall planting. The spokesperson will inform listeners not only what to buy to prepare for those beautiful spring gardens but <u>where</u> to buy the best mulch and bulbs in the industry. There will also be Thanksgiving and, of course, Easter themes. ¶ In addition, we will provide Garden World Nurseries with frequent mention in many local newspaper columns, particularly Frank Darby's column in <u>The New York Times</u>. There is also the strong possibility that Garden World Nurseries will play an important role in the very popular television show, <u>Gardening with Lily</u>, hosted by Lily Richards, the well-known tulip specialist. Hopewell would like to see Garden World Nurseries' products, plants, and logo displayed throughout the wide tri-state area viewing audience. ¶ As you can see, Ms. Jackson, Hopewell Associates has ideas, winning ideas, for Garden World Nurseries. I am enclosing our brochure as well as our impressive client list to give you a sense of our range and versatility. I will be calling in a few days to discuss these ideas with you. ¶ Sincerely ■ Mark Rogers ■ Account Executive ■ Enclosure *200+ words*

New Key Drill

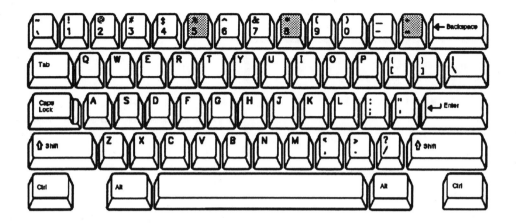

Left Hand
5 ■ Use F finger

Right Hand
8 ■ Use K finger
= ■ Use ; finger

Practice each new reach several times. Then keyboard these practice lines:

```
k kk kkk kik ki8 8 88 888 k8k 888 8k8

f ff fff frf fr5 5 55 555 f5f 555 5f5

; ;; ;;; ;p; ;p= = == === ;=; === =;=
```

Accuracy Development

After 8 p.m., there were 80 automobiles en route.

Of the 55 runners included in the race, 50 faded.

The = symbol is most often called the equal sign.

8 - 5 = 3; 85 - 80 = 5; 58 - 38 = 20; 17 - 9 = 8.

Precision Optical, Inc.
810 South Sienna Street
Fort Worth, TX 76131-8377
1-800-555-3287 ⬤ Fax 1-817-555-7236

July 22, 19--

Ms. Hannah Markum
Technical Systems Manager
Wellington Laboratories, Inc.
1414 Northwest Parkway
Seattle, WA 98121-7483

Dear Ms. Markum

We would like to announce the availability of our T-2983 lens series for your Tekno microscopes. I am enclosing a brochure that includes all the details you need about this exciting new laboratory tool.

The long testing period has determined that the T-2983 lenses will outlast the WX-38 lens series. The lenses were tested at the University of Maryland Medical School and at Bridley Hospital in Texas. After a full year of daily use in research and clinical labs, the lenses performed perfectly.

Most fluorescent microscopes show certain amounts of image degradation after one to two years of use. Labs across the country have contributed their findings to our development effort. We believe that our product will solve many research problems.

Upgrading to the new lens series is quick and easy. As with the older T-100 series, these lenses can be used with your existing flourescent

---

Ms. Hannah Markum
Page 2
July 22, 19-- ↓ 3

microscopes and with any new equipment you may purchase. Your Precision Optical representative will help you design a plan to ensure equipment compatibility in the future.

Quantity orders can be processed with site discounts. We are also prepared to offer half-hour training assistance at sites not using our T-100 lens series. Requests for a demonstration session should be directed to Alan Malik.

We appreciate your interest in the T-2983 lens series. We believe these lenses represent a true advance in laboratory equipment.

Please call if you need further information about these powerful new research tools.

Sincerely

PRECISION OPTICAL, INC.

James E. Jannson

James E. Jannson
Hospital Accounts

ep

Enclosure

If you must use two pages for a letter, follow all the normal rules for the format you are using. At the bottom of page 1:

- Leave approximately 1 inch of space for the bottom margin.

- You can end page 1 at the end of a paragraph. If you must break a paragraph, don't leave a single line by itself at the bottom of the page. Keep at least 2 lines of a paragraph on the first page. Also, begin page 2 with at least 2 lines of the paragraph that is being broken.

For page 2:

- Use a plain sheet (not letterhead).

- Space down 1 inch from the top of the second page.

- At the left margin, type the addressee's name. Return once and type the page number (use the word *Page*); then return and type the date.

- Return two or three times after the heading and continue the letter. *Note:* Triple-spacing is shown.

Power Building

Long-range forecasting indicates an 8 percent decrease in the amount of automobile sales in 1995. This figure is based on the formula $F = 158 - 3x$. Do we recommend that production in our extrusions plant be discontinued by October 8 or December 5?

In our last-minute changes, we forgot to insert a provision for the 8 p.m. guest speaker. He is 85 years old on Friday, and perhaps 15 minutes could be added in order to serve cake to the 95 guests. Is this possible? Call 359-7128 and let Jo know.

Speed Timing

In the formula $xy - ab$, should we consider $b = 15$ or 18? Our new instructions are not clear enough to distinguish between b and/or h. If $b = 18$, we can expect considerable variations in the answer, which will offset our forecast for the year 2000.
--1----2----3----4----5----6----7----8----9---10-

LESSON 15 : ■ Keyboard Review

Keyboard each group of practice lines twice with single-spacing. Return twice after each group.

Review

She awoke at the crack of dawn eager to start her long day of work on the brand-new movie her group was making about a young girl who went to Africa. As she got started, however, the hazy sun created problems with a video recorder and other cameras.

Kim, the engineer/technician, assured us that the difficulty could be quickly corrected by rotating violet left-side control knobs one-fourth or more to the right. Also, he suggests we protect every lens from the effect of haze or high temperature.

3 ■ *Form 5-3* ■ *Proofread this letter.*

Use a comma ■ Review comma rules and use commas correctly. Commas allow for accurate, smooth reading. Incorrect punctuation makes it difficult for your reader to concentrate on the message.

Remember two general rules: Use a comma only where a comma is needed. If a comma is not needed, do not insert one. Never insert a comma just to indicate a pause.

Comma rules are included in the English review on pages 105-106. Take a minute now to review these rules. Then proofread the letter below, which includes several comma errors. Also look for misspellings and capitalization mistakes.

State abbreviations ■ The official U.S. Postal Service list of state abbreviations is provided on page 103.

```
Sptember 18, 19--



Mr. Marsha Bartlett
Northeast Education Srvices, Inc.
42, Williston Rod
burlington, Vt.  05401-7755

Dear Ms. Barlett:

Thank you for giving us the opportunity, to come into your
office and show you our new management accounting program.
We really appreciate, your taking the time to review the
system and, attend the training class.

As we mentioned in the class Quick-Account has a lot of
advantages in the classroom.  It has been equally successful,
with high school students and with adults.  A short, tutorial
shows students how to use the special function keys--they
never have to open a book before they get started.  That
means you, the teacher can focus your attention on
applications.  You will see, results fast!

We can provide Quick-Account as a true production system and
we can also supply a short educational version.  Your system
will include a set of workbooks, a teacher's reference guide
and a disk with student projects.  A full year of free
software support is included in the basic price of $1,250.
If you compare the value of our system we think you will
choose Quick-Account.

Please let us know, if we can provide further information.
We look forward to hearing from you again.
```

New Reach Drill

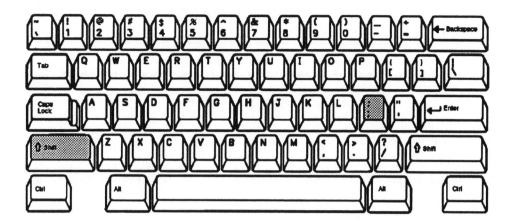

Right Hand
: ■ Use ; finger

Make the new reach several times, and keyboard this practice:

```
;:; ;:; 1:00, 3:59, 5:28, Dear Ms. Red:
```

Accuracy Development

Colons will be used in numeric program formats to display the time, as illustrated in an example of 6:30 p.m. or 1:50 a.m. Where 24-hour clocks will be followed, certain times such as 1:00 and 13:00 would mean 1:00 a.m. and 1:00 p.m., respectively.

The basic data program could be prefixed with a 0 on item .0926. Jo should enter each account item to appear as 0.0926.187 instead of .0926.187. To repeat one good rule, remember that whole numbers precede decimals in any computer data processing.

Many programs use a numeric format for entering a date and/or time information. It is true, May 1, 1993, can be keyboarded as 5/1/93; June 30, 1993, could be keyboarded as 6/30/93. The / is now the mark most often used to write or keyboard a date.

Power Building

The rocket launch was on 6/25/92 and dock 8/1/95.

Long bulletins are issued at 10:30 and 11:45 p.m.

David left on 10/23 at 11 a.m. and arrived 10/26.

Keep the date/time entry sent at 10/3/07 - 18:15.

Proofreading for Accuracy

When you finish a document, *always* check the following:

1. Spelling of all personal names.

2. Accuracy of every street address.

3. Spelling of the city name.

4. Accuracy of the state abbreviation.

5. Accuracy of the zip code.

6. Accurate capitalizing of names.

7. Accuracy of dates.

8. Accuracy of punctuation throughout.

9. Accuracy of your corrections!

10. Final corrected version saved in memory, if appropriate.

Everyone knows that errors should be corrected. However, it is not so easy to *find* errors!

Most of us would like to think we don't make mistakes. We don't really want to do work over or spend too much time checking our work. So we are careless when proofreading, and many mistakes are never noticed. *You will stand out in any business situation if you learn to find mistakes.*

1 ■ Check names separately.

Proper nouns (names) must be correctly spelled. Force your eye to stop when you read each proper noun in a document—don't let your eye flow as you would read a sentence. Can you find all five errors in the example below? (Also see Form 5-1.)

Correct original:

Ms. Anne Lemaster
443 Sawyer Road
Salt Lake City, UT 84116-4972

You keyboarded:

Mr. Ann LeMaster
443 Sawyr Road
Salt Lake City, UH 84116-4972

2 ■ Read the body of a document separately.

After you have checked the facts of a document, read the text. Comma errors occur often. Sometimes a comma is misplaced or mistakenly inserted or left out. Can you find the errors in these sentences? (Also see Form 5-2.)

1. We sent the payment but, the shipment has not arrived.

2. The system is working well and we are happy with it.

3. Considering the problems we had I am surprised we finished the job.

Control Development

Dear Ms. Walthorn:

We want to thank the Rural Office for discovering that account 12-137-03 was flagged and considered by First National Savings to be closed because of being inactive since 5/19/83. Please adjust your necessary records at opening time, 8:30, on 8/26.

Have the countdown changed on EXL-914 to commence at 6:30 after each system has been verified as in a ready state. The launch will be rescheduled as planned from 9:30 on 6/12 to 8:45 on 6/15. Would you notify Sue of this change no later than 5/29?

Speed Timing

Bob will enter the date/time at 1/15/94 - 7:30 so the equation ab - 4de = m can be set in rotation, a pattern that is congruent for advanced communications, as in a Plan 2 forecast. If the plan is good, the back-up systems should not be required.
--1----2----3----4----5----6----7----8----9---10-

LESSON 16   ! ■ (■ $ ■)

Keyboard each practice line twice with single-spacing. Return twice after each two-line group.

Review

The 19 flyers accepted 440 for their unit number.

If 90 students score 411 or higher, we shall win.

The scaled reading of 491 is much lower than 940.

Of the 40 women in the race, 19 won large prizes.

```
Speed      Sid did rush an authentic prism to the city for the profit.

Control    Paula Minot grew up in Quincy, Massachusetts, in the 1980s.
```

The simplified format is designed for efficiency. Note these important features:

- No extra keystrokes, such as tabs

- No salutation (especially helpful when addressee name is not known or writer does not want to personalize letter)

- No complimentary close (saves keystrokes)

These advantages are significant in terms of production time saved. However, the format has a somewhat cold appearance. Many people modify the format for a more personal effect. Some may indent the date or subject line. Others add a complimentary close such as *Sincerely yours*, even though a salutation is not used. In this text we show the standard format, but be prepared for individual office style to vary.

The lack of a salutation still allows the advantage of avoiding the awkward salutation of *Dear Sir* or *Ladies and Gentlemen*.

Avoid changing line lengths (margins). Use one setting (either 1" or 1.25" margins).

1 ▪ *Form 4-1* ▪ *Keyboard Example 3.*

Notice how much time is saved by blocking all elements at the left margin and by using a shortened signature block. Use 1" or 1.25" margins.

2 ▪ *Form 4-2* ▪ *Key this letter in the format of Example 3.*

Martinez and Lange, P.A. ▪ 4777 Ocean Boulevard, Suite 19 ▪ Jacksonville, FL 32207-1131 ▪ Change in maintenance policy *(put in all caps)* ▪ Because of increased manufacturing costs and insurance liability, we have had to make adjustments in our maintenance policy. These changes will be in effect at your next contract renewal date. ¶ We can no longer supply loaner equipment at no cost while we repair existing equipment. Beginning at your next contract renewal or January 3, 19--, whichever comes first, a daily charge will be applied for loaner equipment. Leasing can also be arranged through our maintenance department. The charge varies with the equipment involved. ¶ We are also increasing the annual rate for emergency on-site repair. A new base rate of $200 per visit will apply to all emergency maintenance calls to your district sales office. This rate replaces the current $75 rate. ¶ Please note these policy changes and call us if you have further questions. ▪ Andy McGowan--Vice President *(use all caps)* *over 150 words*

3 ▪ *Form 4-3* ▪ *Key this simplified letter.* If you are working at a computer, recall Letter 2 and use the inside address—don't rekey. Rekeying standard information adds time and may cause errors.

Though this letter is short, do not set larger margins. You can save time by using one standard setting.

[Use inside address from preceding letter.] ▪ VOICE MAIL PROCEDURES ▪ Our new voice mail system is designed to suit your busy practice. Messages of almost any length can be left 24 hours a day. ¶ To access the service, simply dial our switchboard. Then respond to the series of questions as requested. ¶ Our system is also equipped with an emergency feature. In an emergency, press # immediately after the recorded message begins. You will be connected with the service department. Dial phone users can dial 0 immediately to report an emergency. ▪ [Use signature line from previous letter.] ▪ Enclosure: Procedures card *under 100 words*

New Reach Drill

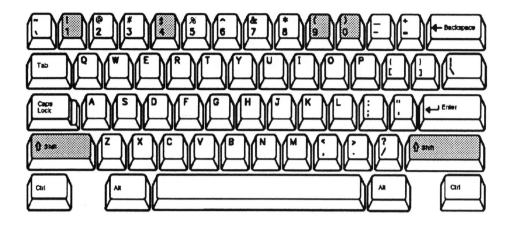

Left Hand
! ■ Use A finger
$ ■ Use F finger

Right Hand
(■ Use L finger
) ■ Use ; finger

Practice each new reach several times. Then keyboard these practice lines:

aaa ;;; aq! aq! ask ask! also also!

lll aaa lo(lo(slo(slo((flo (flo

;;; fff fr$ fr$ $88 $40 $30 $91 $72

aaa ;;; ;p) ;p) ap) ap) flap) flap)

Accuracy Development

Stop those thieves! Bring them here immediately!

Did you notice that the book is two dollars ($2)?

She (Mary, that is) contributed $50 to the cause.

Ed presents the following advice: (1) Think big!
(2) Stick to one meaningful goal! (3) Go for it!

Amundsen & Davis

Hospital Suppliers
9620 West Colorado Street
Chicago, IL 60614-5583
1-800-555-7365

July 10, 19-- ↓4

Sinai Children's Hospital
1855 91st Street
New York, NY 10024-5736 ↓3

ESTIMATE FOR REHABILITATION EQUIPMENT ↓3   ←takes place of salutation

I am enclosing our revised quotation for three MYCOFLEX
surge-protected muscular rehabilitation units. This
quotation reflects the addition of a treadmill with
electronic monitoring. This equipment can be installed
within two weeks of your order, provided the order is placed
before August 5.

You may want to install a system-override switch to allow
individual control of the separate units. The additional
cost for this feature is listed on the quotation.

We look forward to providing you with these effective units
and with continuing maintenance service. Rates for
maintenance are provided separately on the quote. ↓4

Terry Price

MS. TERRY PRICE   ←writer name and title can be placed on one line
CUSTOMER SERVICE   (name and title are then separated by a comma or dash)

st

Enclosure   ←enclosures don't have to be named in any format

cc Frank Whitcomb, Sales Manager

Example 3
Simplified Letter

Power Building

In the group, four (JoAnn, Rod, Mary, and Al) are
considered to be very much the most likely to win
a big $5,000 scholarship. Five thousand dollars!
That is really a lot of money, but in the economy
of today, such amounts cannot buy you everything.

Did Jay consider a change in automatic pagination
(Documents 6-19) to stop after pages 285 and 286,
if possible? Important information then appears:
(1) social security number, (2) employment dates,
(3) date of birth, and (4) $1,000 or $5,000 sums.

Speed Timing

Entry time yesterday (4:30) appeared to be satisfactory to many new operators, who were given the
scaled wage of $6.50 per hour. However, some who
were paid on the line-count basis expressed to Jo
that they were victims of unfair practice! Help!
--1----2----3----4----5----6----7----8----9---10-

LESSON 17   @ ■ & ■ # ■ _ ■ Backspace

Note: In this lesson, you learn how to underscore. If you are using a computer,
you will use the *underline* function instead of the backspace feature with the
underscore key. Be sure you know how to underline on your system.

Keyboard this group of practice lines twice with single-spacing. Return twice
after the group.

Review

Total winnings (lottery) were $273,000 yesterday!
Many of the winners chose 47 as the winning card.
State-of-the-art procedures involved smart clues.
Did your group (73) have any winners? Ask David.

```
Speed      She lent me the pen and bicycle to go to town with the key.

Control    Allan, tell the bookkeepers to close the yellow door fully.
```

1 ■ *Form 3-1* ■ *Key Example 2.* ■ *You will need to set a tab at the center point.*

Set center tab ■

Typewriter (10 pitch): Clear all tabs (at each tab, press Tab Clear). You have 85 spaces on the line. Set a tab at the halfway point (42).

Typewriter (12 pitch): Clear all tabs (at each tab, press Tab Clear). You have 102 spaces on the line. Set a tab at the halfway point (51).

Computer: Clear all tabs. On the text screen, give center command. Note position number of cursor. Delete center command and set an absolute tab at this position. (Set a Left Tab at this point.)

2 ■ *Form 3-2* ■ *Key this letter in the format of Example 2.*

Addressee name not known ■ Sometimes you will not know the name of the person you are writing to, but you still have to include a salutation in the block and modified block formats.

The old-fashioned *Dear Sir:* is no longer popular, but the other choices are not much better. In this text we recommend the use of *Ladies and Gentlemen.* However, you should be aware that business practice varies on this point. Be prepared to follow office style.

R & B Exhibits, Inc. ■ 355 Craign Highway ■ Indianapolis, IN 46323-1771 ■ Ladies and Gentlemen: ■ We will be exhibitors at the December medical conference at the Conference Center. This year we would like to arrange for a larger booth area and for cellular phone service. We would also like to have extra 220V electrical outlets in our booth. ¶ In addition, please make

every effort to provide increased security for the exhibits this year. We are bringing some extremely expensive computer equipment. Last year the exhibit area was supposed to have security service at all times. However, our representatives were able to pass through the doors to the exhibits late at night, and no guard was present. This arrangement is not satisfactory to us. ¶ Please provide specific details on exhibit room security in our contract. We also request that you consider the possibility of locking the exhibit area promptly at 5 p.m. both days of the exhibit. We cannot afford to lose this equipment. ¶ We had a successful exhibit overall, however, and we are looking forward to taking part in this year's meeting. Thank you for your help in making our arrangements. ■ Sincerely yours, ■ APEX SOFTWARE, INC. ■ Caryn Matthews ■ Exhibits Coordinator ■ cc: Rob Gino, Sales Manager
160 words

3 ■ *Form 3-3* ■ *Key this letter in Example 2 format.*

Ms. Janet Robb [use R & B Exhibits inside address as in letter 2] ■ Dear Ms. Robb: ■ Thank you for faxing me your standard contract for the December convention at the Indianapolis Conference Center. I was able to review the new security provisions quickly. For the most part, these new procedures should be a big improvement on the arrangements of last year. ¶ However, we still believe that the exhibit room should be locked at the end of exhibit hours. Last year, several exhibitors lost software sometime between 5 p.m. and 8 a.m., when exhibits reopened. I think you will have many grateful exhibitors if you make the room off-limits when exhibits close. ¶ Please let me know how you decide on this important issue. A faxed response will be fine. ■ [Use signature block and *cc* notation as for preceding letter.] *100 words*

New Reach Drill

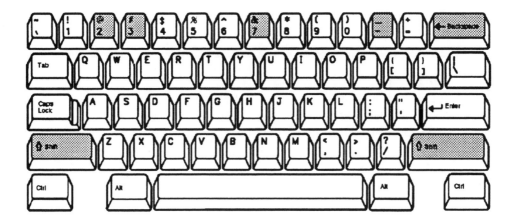

Left Hand	**Right Hand**
@ ■ Use S finger	& ■ Use J finger
# ■ Use D finger	_ ■ Use ; finger
	Backspace ■ Use ; finger

Underline. To **underline** with a typewriter, type the letters to be underscored. Then backspace and type the underscore. Practice each new reach, and then keyboard these practice lines:

```
sss ;;; sw@ sw@ s@s s@s four @ .10

jjj aaa ju& ju& j&J j&J one & four

ddd ;;; de# de# d#d d#d #750 2900#

;;; aaa ;p_ ;p_ ;_; ;_; ___ ___ __

We paid $250 for equipment in May.
```

Note: In determining word counts for underlined words **at a typewriter**, count 1 letter + 1 backspace + 1 underscore = 3 strokes per underlined letter.

At a computer, count 1 stroke for turning on underline and 1 stroke for turning it off.

APEX SOFTWARE, INC.
8510 Woodhaven Boulevard
Flushing, NY 11341-0039
Phone 1-800-555-7334 Fax 718-555-3874

[tab to center]   June 22, 19-- ↓4

Mr. Will MacGregor
Tinley Products, Inc.
455 West State Street
Wilmont, NY 10034-5477

Dear Mr. MacGregor: ←note punctuation

As I mentioned on the phone last week, we received your fax
transmission stating that we have a past due balance of
$1,557.99 in our company account (No. AM65-3303-76). I
thought the total balance had been paid, but I wanted to take
time to check our records.

Please check your files for our check No. 4454, which was
written and sent on June 5 in full payment of the balance
due. I am enclosing a photocopy of the canceled check, which
shows your endorsement clearly on the back, and a photocopy
of your receipt of June 9.

I believe these documents will allow you to correct your
records. Please let me know if you need further information
about this account.↓2

[tab to center]   Cordially, ↓2

[tab to center]   APEX SOFTWARE, INC. ↓4

                                             Sandra B. Norris

                                             Sandra B. Norris
                                             Vice President

hr

Enclosures: Copy of canceled check and receipt

cc: Ray Gurr, Accounting

Example 2
Modified Block Letter
Mixed Punctuation

Accuracy Development

Loss of five disks @ $200 totals the same as this
loss of four @ $250. Order me five disks @ $200.

R & A Garage uses Hendershot, Piece & Wheelwright
mechanics for complicated alignment or balancing.

Place an order for ten #30-794-VT Word Processing
Stations @ $2,000. The unit weight could be 20#.

The $2,000 per unit cost might be for #30-794-VTA
only and does not include this 20# shipping cost.

Power Building

Several team members (Bart, Al & Rod) agreed that
#747 could be eliminated from the advanced course
requirement and said 20# paper will be purchased.
The cost for standard-size 20# bond was 5 reams @
$5.50 or 10 reams @ $5.25. Tell them the choice.

None of the software problems are attributable to
scratches on the #18-37-HD. Apex has been called
and may run diagnostics A & B to determine if the
skip problem is now associated with the hard disk
and/or the newly installed 7# communications box.

Speed Timing

On March 2, we purchased one hundred-twenty (120)
#43-978-WX for use in the law offices of Gatling,
Remington & Smith. Our company issued check #870
on April 5 for $240,000 (120 #43-978-WX @ $2,000)
in accordance with the terms quoted on January 9.
--1----2----3----4----5----6----7----8----9---10-

office support staff is having a hard time using the special commands needed for simple functions. I hope you can provide some guidance in making this installation smoother for us. ¶ It was very helpful to have the remote hook-up yesterday. I'm not sure what you did, but the changes certainly made a big difference in the computer processing speed. ■ Sincerely ■ Ms. Kyle Fossler ■ Operations ■ Enclosures: Printouts ■ cc: Ms. Kathy Martin *130 words*

3 ■ *Form 2-3* ■ *Example 1 as model* ■ *6" or 6.5" line*

Prepare the handwritten letter below. You can find the address of Northeast SoftWare, Inc., earlier in this lesson.

Reading handwritten copy ■ If you are keying from a handwritten draft, be aware of a few potential problems. First, handwriting is almost always harder to read than typed or printed material.

Take time to read every word. Check for spelling errors and apply punctuation rules. The writer may carelessly write a period that looks like a comma. Use common sense when you work from this kind of draft.

People who are writing by hand often abbreviate words. Spell out abbreviated terms unless you are told otherwise.

Subject line ■ In block format, the subject line appears flush left, two lines below the salutation.

```
Dear Mr. Clary ↓2

Subject:  Project ER 1002 ↓2

Please review your . . .
```

---

from the desk of **Kathy Martin**

Dear Stan

Subject: Training Sessions

The dates for the software training sessions have finally been selected. We would like your trainers to schedule Oct. 9-10 for our full-day sessions. The half-day session will take place on Oct. 13. You can expect 21 people in each session. The "students" will include our operations vice president and most of our administrative support staff.

We're all looking forward to the classes. Thank you for being so flexible about the schedule.

Sincerely yours

Please address this letter to Stan Clary at Northeast Soft Ware, Inc.
— Kathy

LESSON 18

Keyboard each group of lines twice with single-spacing. Return twice after each group.

Review

Invoice #62 indicated 91 tapes @ $15 were shipped from Atlanta System Office Support on December 3.

Assure that my total shipment weight will not exceed the approved truck express allowance of 50#.

New Reach Drill

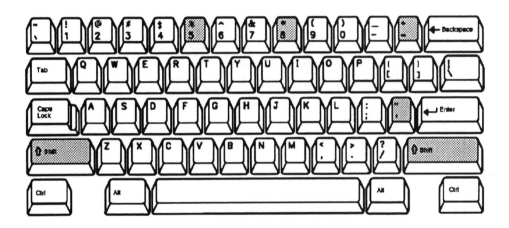

Left Hand
% ■ Use F finger

Right Hand
* ■ Use K finger
+ ■ Use ; finger
" ■ Use ; finger

Practice each new reach, and then keyboard these practice lines:

aaa kkk ki* ki* k*k k*k note* *see

fff ;;; fr% fr% f%f f%f 90% 3% 75%

;;; aaa ;;+ ;;+ ;+; ;+; a + b = 80

aaa ;;; ;;" ;;" ;"; ;"; "Sam" "Al"

Key these drill lines as described on page 61. Don't forget to check for errors.

Speed   The big man may fix the rosy chair and then enamel it pale.

Control   The Staten Island Ferry carries Dan across New York Harbor.

1 ▪ *Form 2-1* ▪ *Use the full block format (Example 1) to key this letter. Since the letter length is average, use a 6" line (1.25" margins) or a 6.5" line (1" margins).*

Enclosure notation ▪ An enclosure notation tells the reader that materials are included with the letter. (The materials are also mentioned within the letter itself.)

```
Dick Grenson, Jr.
President

am ↓2


Enclosure:   Member List
           ↑ 2 spaces after colon
```

Mr. Stan Clary ▪ Northeast SoftWare, Inc. ▪ 181 Hasting Road ▪ Portland, ME 04106-5403 ▪ Dear Mr. Clary ▪ Thank you for sending the materials I requested on the phone last week. I received the preview disk yesterday, and I have spent most of the morning trying to learn about preparing graphics. I like the program very much. ¶ I am recommending that we buy the enhanced version of your software for our staff here at the office. I am also suggesting that we buy additional copies of the standard version for use by our consultants, who usually work at home on their own equipment. Can you please let me know if we will have any trouble running the software on both IBM-compatible equipment and Macintosh machines? ¶ In addition, I am sending you a printout of my attempt to create pie charts. As you will see, I had problems shading the largest section. What am I doing wrong? This

example was printed on a Poly IIIe laser printer. ¶ Please give me a call when convenient to answer these questions. We are on a tight deadline (as always), and I am eager to place an order. ▪ Sincerely yours ▪ Kathy Martin ▪ Communications ▪ Enclosure: Pie chart
160 words

2 ▪ *Form 2-2* ▪ *Format model: Use Example 1.* ▪ *6" or 6.5" line*

Copy notation ▪ The copy notation appears last, as shown here. Sometimes *c* is used instead of *cc*. Space twice after the colon. The colon may be omitted. If no colon is used, space once after the *cc* or *c*.

```
am

Enclosure:   Map

cc:  Ms. Dora Henry
```

Writer's identification for woman ▪ Often a courtesy title is included in the signature block (writer's identification) if the writer is a woman, especially if her first name can also be a man's.

Mr. Stan Clary ▪ Northeast SoftWare, Inc. ▪ 181 Hasting Road ▪ Portland, ME 04106-5403 ▪ Dear Stan ▪ As you will see from the enclosed laser printout, the formats for our displays are not yet working as planned. Please look over the steps I noted and provide an explanation of the problems. ¶ I am not a technical expert, but I believe that the initial input should be easier for those of us who don't know computers! Our

Accuracy Development

Some of my software programs contained rote* memories using the procedure aa + b + cc + dd + eee.

Nearly 7% of the vendors preferred service by the XY Corporation on their Model #72-851-A memories.

Determining which modem* we chose created several signal problems, according to "Big Tony" (<u>Chief</u>).

Using the * in <u>Program</u> #862 means to print "Enter your name" instead of "Type your account number."

Power Building

If 6 + 9 = 15, our readings on the <u>Bentley</u> scales should be adjusted to reflect the change (+ or -) by 15 to accommodate varied* temperature fluctuations. Normally an 18% tolerance will enable the "cracking" test pressures to increase 75# or 85#.

Speed Timing

Numerous "boot" faults in #22-86-BZO "mods" cause us to have serious doubts about whether the software is "clean" enough for our operations. These 55% of your* mods contained 9 or more faults, indicating the <u>inferior</u> quality control conditions.
--1----2----3----4----5----6----7----8----9---10-

LESSON 19   ' ■ Shift Lock ■ Review

Keyboard each practice line twice with single-spacing. Return twice after each two-line group.

Review

Elizabeth will set the Mylar* setting at + or -2.

Yesterday the cost of energy was 23% of the norm.

"Big Foot" was the favored myth* in <u>Program</u> #795.

Send the 5,000# shipment of red candy to Altoona.

Reading the copy ■ The paragraph sign (¶) means to begin a new paragraph. Double-space between paragraphs. The approximate number of words in the body of the letter is shown at the end. This number will be of use to you later, when you set line lengths yourself for long or short letters. For now, line length settings are provided.

End-of-line hyphens ■ Avoid hyphenating. If you have to break a word at the end of a line, place the hyphen correctly. Check a dictionary if you are not sure. Don't hyphenate the first line of a letter, and never hyenate more than three lines in a row.

Dictionary ■ A dictionary normally shows a centered dot to show appropriate hyphen locations for entry words, as in *hy•phen•ate*.

Mr. Charles M. Merks ■ 1522 Fenworth Building ■ Pittsburgh, PA 15232-1522 ■ Dear Mr. Merks ■ Thank you for agreeing to do everything you can to speed up delivery of our letterheads and laser printer paper. We were already on a tight deadline when we placed the order, but today we were told the deadline has been changed. We now have fewer than three weeks to prepare a mailing to our 1,500 stockholders. I can't believe we can make it, but we're going to try! ¶ Please ship the order via overnight express, as we discussed. I understand that shipping is prepaid by you and included on our invoice. ¶ I appreciate your help. After this project is over, I want to learn more about your laser printer specialty papers. We are investigating the possibility of desktop publishing for company announcements. ■ Sincerely yours ■ GRENSON ACCOUNTING CONSULTANTS ■ Wanda Parker ■ Office Manager
130 words (approx.)

3 ■ *Form 1-3* ■ *Type this letter in Example 1 format.* ■ *Because it is short, use a line of approximately 5 inches (margins set at 2").*

Title in inside address ■ In the inside address, the person's title is used (President). A short title can be placed at the end of the first line (use a comma before the title) or on the second line of the inside address. Use the more balanced-looking placement.

Mr. William Bonita, President ■ Southwest Data, Inc. ■ 4245 Vallahandra Drive ■ Irvine, CA 90027 ■ Dear Mr. Bonita ■ The forms provided by General Movies International, our client, seem to be out of date. Our representative told me over the phone today that the current forms are on the way. We expect to receive them on Tuesday. After our project team looks them over, we'll fax you copies of the forms you need. ¶ I expect your work on this project can proceed without delay after we receive the correct forms. We're still hoping for a completion date early next month. ■ Sincerely ■ GRENSON ACCOUNTING CONSULTANTS ■ Carl Hawes ■ Project Contact   *75 words*

4 ■ *Form 1-4* ■ *Key this letter using Example 1 as a format guide.* ■ *Use a 5-inch line.*

Extra space above date ■ Leave extra space above the date if necessary to balance a very short letter on the page. *Computer*: Place the date 3½ or 4 inches down from the top of the page. *Typewriter*: Use 20 to 24 returns before the date.

Ms. Kathy Lutz-Williamson, Operations Manager ■ Rocky Mountain Transport ■ 16 Colfax Avenue ■ Denver, CO 80201-0016 ■ Dear Ms. Lutz-Williamson ■ Our preliminary review of your documents is now complete. Thank you for supplying complete information. ¶ I do not expect to have any problem preparing a detailed proposal within two weeks. You should have our proposal in your hands well before the preliminary deadline you suggested. ¶ Thank you for giving us the opportunity to submit a proposal. ■ Sincerely yours ■ GRENSON ACCOUNTING CONSULTANTS ■ Dick Grenson, Jr. ■ President
50 words

New Reach Drill

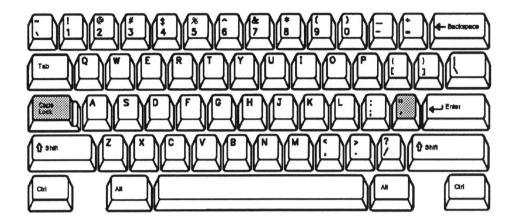

Left Hand   **Right Hand**

Shift (Caps) Lock ■ Use A finger   ' ■ Use ; finger

Note: The Shift Lock or Caps Lock may be on the right side of your keyboard. If so, use the ; finger to press this key.

Practice each new reach, and then keyboard these practice lines:

;; ;'; ;'; ''' ''' ';' ';' a's d's

aaa JIFFY 111; Library "A LIBRARY"

Accuracy Development

Bob's report indicated several departments' books were not balanced with the company's '92 account.

To keyboard alphabetic information or data in ALL CAPITAL LETTERS, follow the SHIFT LOCK procedure.

Please send your 94 formula (A + B) x 8 = (C + D) to PROJECT ZEBRA for determining (X - Y)/60 data.

Speed	It is their duty to work for big pay with us and make pens.
Control	All Americans value vegetables from the San Joaquin Valley.

Letter Placement. Each letter assignment tells you the approximate number of words in the body of a letter. You can use this figure to determine your production typing rate. (Divide the approximate number of words by the number of minutes it took to type the letter.)

You should also note whether a letter is short (up to 100 words), average (from 100 to 150 words), or long (over 150 words). In most cases, a short letter should have a short line. An average line setting is 6 inches (side margins of 1¼ inches). Average and long letters are often prepared with a 6½-inch line because this is the standard setting on word processing software and electronic typewriters.

Length	*Line*	*Margins*	*Settings*	
			10-pitch	*12-pitch*
Short	5" (approx.)	2.00"	20–65	24–78
Average	6"	1.25"	13–73	21–81
Long	6.5"	1"	10–75	18–83

Your working folder contains four letterheads like that shown for Example 1. Use the form that matches the number after each assignment.

1 ■ *Form 1-1 ■ Key Example 1.*

In the sample letter, note the salutation and the complimentary close. Open punctuation and mixed punctuation are both acceptable (but use open punctuation here).

Open punctuation: **Dear Peter ■ Sincerely**

Mixed punctuation: **Dear Peter: ■ Sincerely,**

Placement ■ Type the date 2.5 inches from the top of the page (15 lines down on a typewriter). After typing the date, return 4 times. Then key the inside address. Leave 1 or 2 spaces before the zip code in the last line of the inside address. (This text shows 2 spaces before the zip code.)

Double-space after the complimentary close and key the company identification line. Then return 4 times and key the writer's name.

Signature ■ Always allow 4 returns for the writer's signature. What if the company identification line is left out? You simply return 4 times after the complimentary close.

2 ■ *Form 1-2 ■ Use Example 1 as a format guide for the following letter.*

The letter is approximately the same length as the sample letter. If you completed Letter 1 correctly, you will use the same placement for the date and inside address here.

Date and Initials. Use today's date. Key your own initials (lowercase) as the typist. (Do the same for all assignments in Level 3.)

Power Building

Several of us "girls" went to Evelyn's Restaurant for the seafood buffet, whereas some of us wanted prime rib and rode the extra two miles to Momma's Place. At Momma's, the PRIME RIB SPECIAL is only $5.50 for those presenting the coupon with #50PR.

Keep track of (CD + AB) = (E + F)/10 for programming the orbital pattern of "Lab Star" when JUNTO blips on your radar at approximately 5:00 on 9/2. Do <u>not</u> depress the red STOP CONTROL if (E + F)/10 values exceed (CD + AB). STOP only if reading 3.

Speed Timing

Satellite communication via microwave emitted red X-ray images that will NOT be removed by applying the (BC - D)/4 = (AE + 20) formulas. Each set of computational data reveals <u>slight</u> color variances from 10% or 15% at the .5 level of color density.
--1----2----3----4----5----6----7----8----9---10-

✓ **Keyboard Complete**

This is the final lesson on the computer or typewriter keyboard. Other keys not yet covered are used for special equipment functions. You will learn to use these keys as you apply your skills in typing or word processing jobs (Level 3).

You are now ready to develop your keyboarding ability into a real skill. You might proceed to Level 2, which is invaluable for helping increase your speed and accuracy. Your instructor may ask you to proceed directly to applications in Level 3. If so, take time to return to a lesson in Level 2 every other day or every three days. These lessons are specially designed to build your skill.

GRENSON ACCOUNTING CONSULTANTS
2236 MARAHIELO DRIVE
LOS ANGELES, CA 90017-8830

↓2.5" or line 15
April 27, 19-- ↓4   ← date

Mr. Peter Auberge, Director   ← inside address
ASC Maritime Research Agency
111 Hanley Plaza
San Jacinto, CA 95401-7383 ↓2

Dear Peter ↓2   ← salutation

I wanted to let you know that we received your supplement to
the San Jacinto University Whale Stock Research Project. It
looks as if it will help us come up with more accurate cost
estimates for leasing the research vessel.

I can appreciate the pressure the University is placing on
you, and I assure you that we expect to meet the deadline for
submitting the financial feasibility report. I have given it
the highest priority here.

I look forward to seeing you at the University Trustees'
meeting on Friday.

Sincerely ↓2   ← complimentary close

GRENSON ACCOUNTING CONSULTANTS ↓4   ← company identification line (optional)

Dick Grenson, Jr.
Dick Grenson, Jr.   ← writer's identification
President ↓2

am   ← preparer's initials

Example 1
Full Block Letter
Open Punctuation
Line length: 6½ inches
Letter length: Average

2
BUILD KEYBOARDING CONTROL

In this section you will find a set of lessons that develop keyboarding control. Control helps you build accuracy and speed in all keyboarding applications.

Most students should complete the Level 2 lessons in order directly after finishing Level 1. Follow the directions carefully to gain the most benefit from Level 2.

After you complete Level 2, you will work on letters, memos, and other projects. Return to a lesson in Level 2 at least once a day and type a passage for 3 to 5 minutes. This repetitive practice will help you build keyboarding control skills fast—and that means rapidly increasing speed and accuracy.

Correct Errors—By Not Making Them!

Today's computers and typewriters make it easy to correct errors as you keyboard (see your equipment manual for correction methods). Even so, correcting mistakes takes time, and most people find it difficult to find all their own errors. Sooner or later, mistakes find their way into letters, reports, and other materials. Making corrections takes a lot of time and energy.

Take time *now* to learn how to correct keystroking mistakes:

- transposed letters, as in *keybaord*

- doubled letters, as in *writingg*

- incorrect letters, as in *oceam*

- omitted letters, as in *beter*

- extra space between words, as in *saw him*

- omitted space between words, as in *wasgone*

- inaccurate punctuation, as in *U,S. history*

- wrong case, as in *Greg phillips* or *my Room*

- incorrect spacing, as with margins, tabs, or "hard" returns

To correct a keystroking error, locate the error and then keyboard the correct version several times—until your fingers "memorize" the keystroke.

3
APPLY YOUR SKILLS

Applying Your Skills

Level 3 focuses on *practice*. You will learn how to prepare essential business documents—letters, memos, envelopes, and other special materials.

Concentrate on each document you prepare. When you finish a letter, study the letter and locate the areas where the format is incorrect or where you've made keying errors. You will progress much more quickly if you make a careful check of the errors in your work.

Quality counts. The jobs in Level 3 emphasize these essentials of quality:

- Accuracy of copy

- Speed of production

- Clean, balanced appearance of document

Building Your Skills

In Level 2, you worked toward improving accuracy and speed. Now you will continue that work as you also consider the appearance of the final product. A message that has a clean and balanced appearance is more likely to be read. This level provides several handy guidelines for preparing attractive materials.

Most lessons in Level 3 include two drill sentences. These sentences are designed to help you improve your skills.

The warm-up sentence is designed for high speed—all words are balanced-hand words. The second line stresses control as you key either capitals, figures, or double letters. Each day, begin with the drill sentences.

Speed: Type 3 times, trying for top speed.

Control: Type 3 times, trying for perfect accuracy.

Final: Check the accuracy of your typed Control sentence. If you made an error, type the sentence 2 more times.

Try to build your speed by 5 words per minute every day you practice.

Building Accuracy. This procedure will help you improve your accuracy. Assume that you keyed an error like this:

```
We are opening our mew season today.
```

To correct the error, type the following once or twice:

```
new new new our new our new our new season
```

If you make a spacing error like that in the first line below, correct the error as shown in the second line:

```
today,and we are glad to be invited.

, , , today, today, today, today, and today, and
```

Follow these steps in Level 2 to build accuracy and speed:

- **Warm-Up Practice (5 minutes)** *single-space; space twice between groups* ■ The copy builds your ability to keyboard with an even touch. Type each line 2 or 3 times each. Don't hurry—your goal is to use correct technique.

- **Fast-Paced Drill (5 minutes daily)** *single-space; space twice between groups* ■ Work at your maximum rate. If you are keyboarding accurately at 30 wpm, try to force your speed up to 35 wpm for a short timing. Try short timings.

- **Attention Drill (5 to 10 minutes daily)** *single-space; space twice after each group; 5-space tab* ■ Most letters of the alphabet are used in each of these drills. Unusual names and other words are included here to help you train yourself to read carefully. Concentrate on accuracy. Accurate reading leads to accurate keyboarding.

- **Speed-Building Practice (5 to 10 minutes daily)** *double-space; indent paragraphs 5 spaces; 5-space tab* ■ The paragraphs for continuous keyboarding are carefully graded. Start each of these sections at your normal keyboarding rate. Then try hard to increase your rate gradually. If you complete the practice before time is up, start over at the beginning.

- **Find and Correct Errors (10 to 15 minutes daily)** ■ When time is up, check your work carefully for errors. Then follow the steps shown earlier to correct your keystroking.

Attention Drill

Have you ever heard the old expression "curiosity killed the cat"? Most of us wouldn't agree that curiosity is a bad quality. If not for curiosity, for example, perhaps the original American "Indians" would not have crossed the land passage near present-day Alaska and wandered the entire length of North and South America. If not for curiosity, we wouldn't have Edison's light bulb or Bell's telephone. Often curiosity is the victor over fear--fear of the unknown or fear of failure. Perhaps the old saying should be changed to "nosiness killed the cat."

Speed-Building Practice

Efficient workers are always aiming for accuracy the first time they complete a project. They remember not to take anything for granted. If a zip code does not look correct, they will take the time to check the number. Common sense is another quality all workers would do well to develop. Everyone knows a story about someone who is smart but has no common sense. The most important goals must always be kept in mind. Productive workers like to finish work in the shortest possible time, and common sense with accuracy helps them meet their goals.

Keep Building Speed and Accuracy

Good speed and accuracy will save a lot of your time and effort in the future. Continue to build speed and accuracy as you apply your keyboarding skills in the assignments of Level 3.

Push for higher speed and accuracy. Every few days, return to a lesson in Level 2 and repeat a practice section. You will be pleased to see how your skills improve with practice.

Remember to check your work for errors. Do not count any timing that has five or more errors. Retake the timing until you have fewer than five mistakes.

Lesson Summary

Lessons 20 through 24: Keyboard line for line

Key practice lines exactly as shown. At a typewriter, set a 60-space line. At a computer, the software default margins should be acceptable. Return manually at the end of each line.

Listen for the bell. If you are working at a typewriter, you will hear a tone or beep as the printing point approaches the right margin. This bell alerts you to the need to make a line-ending decision (you have five to seven spaces remaining on the line). Listen for the bell when you complete Lessons 25 through 30 (see below).

Lessons 25 through 30: Make line-ending decisions

Set a 60-space line. At a computer, set a left margin of 1.5 inches and a right margin of 1 inch. As you key, make your own end-of-line decisions. Your instructor will tell you whether to use automatic return (word wrap) or to return manually at the end of the line.

→Set a Tab

At a computer ■ Tab settings are probably already set every half inch (every 5 spaces) across the screen.

Press the Tab Key once to advance for a paragraph indent. (The Tab key probably shows two straight arrows, one pointing left and one pointing right.) If your left margin is at 1", the position indicator should now say 1.5".

At a typewriter ■ To clear existing tab settings, press the Tab Key. At each stop, press Tab Clear. Then return.

At the left margin, press the space bar 5 times. Then press Tab Set. Return again. Press the Tab key once to advance for a paragraph indent.

Attention Drill

Some people find that official buildings or monuments evoke strong feelings and thoughts, and others might prefer to travel alone, far from any manmade structures, to ponder ideas or events that have gone by. For example, tourists flock to Washington, D.C., by the thousands every year to visit national landmarks like the Lincoln Memorial, the Washington Monument, and the various buildings of the Smithsonian Institution. Other people say that they don't need to walk down Pennsylvania Avenue to understand what our national heritage is.

Speed-Building Practice

You may already know the kind of business or organization you want to join over the next few years. The small company can often offer an informal workplace, and you will feel comfortable here if you enjoy working closely with a few people. Small companies often allow swift growth for people who learn their jobs well. Bigger companies must devote more time to managing their operations and can seem more rigid. However, computers now allow small companies to work like big ones, and big companies now try to imitate the flexibility of smaller ones.

LESSON 30   Keyboarding Control

Warm-Up Practice
Right-Hand and Left-Hand Words

dare hunk dress hum east junk west plum ever pink rest hull	12
hypo hulk hook honk hump honk eats ever ease east drab area	24
grate nippy verse union reacts oily sedge holly tests puppy	36
crazed onlook arcade uphill crease pinion braver pump water	48

--1----2----3----4----5----6----7----8----9---10---11---12-

Fast-Paced Drill

You'll enjoy learning this piece of music--I am sure of it.	12
Try your very best to keep your mind on what you are doing.	24
We planted the tomatoes, but after all that work they died.	36
Minor problems resulted when the motors went in for repair.	48

--1----2----3----4----5----6----7----8----9---10---11---12-

Warm-Up Practice
High-Frequency Sequences: Opposite Hands

```
pa os ek cl nd ap ri us so ye th ng le to el nt cy eh al ht      12
lea ted pri nam ive ank hea etu oul att cho don hav sen rit      24
know some kind both same made good long sure with sits able      36
I know from your last call there will be much more I am now      48
--1----2----3----4----5----6----7----8----9---10---11---12-
```

Fast-Paced Drill

```
Thinking should play a big part in every decision you make.      12
I am really looking forward to the chance to meet you soon.      24
Buy two reams of paper before you begin the latest reports.      36
Letters stored on computer disks are not considered copies.      48
--1----2----3----4----5----6----7----8----9---10---11---12-
```

Attention Drill

```
     Business leaders and government officials have noticed      12
that it is better to keep the workplace safe.  Studies have      24
shown that workers can provide the best advice about office      36
or plant safety.  Many companies rely on teams of employees      48
to talk together and suggest improvements, if any.  Workers      60
are less likely to complain if they know they have a chance      72
to bring about change.  Workers should remember, of course,      84
that change can be very expensive.  On the other hand, most      96
employers know that health problems can cause major delays.     108
--1----2----3----4----5----6----7----8----9---10---11---12-
```

Speed-Building Practice

```
     One good way to gain skill in this area is to put your      12
whole mind on your work.  Make it a point to keep out other      24
things that are not part of the skill you want to get.  You      36
will gain skills if you keep your eyes on the page and your      48
thoughts on the book.  As you key, you will see this point.      60
--1----2----3----4----5----6----7----8----9---10---11---12-
```

Attention Drill

The periodic table of elements is a handy tool in the field of chemistry because it contains a listing of elements and shows their relation in groups. Did you know that the first element on the chart is hydrogen? The elements are abbreviated on the table; hydrogen is represented by the letter H. Sodium is shown by the abbreviation Na, while sulfur is shown by an S. Sodium occurs in common substances, like table salt or sodium chloride. Sulfur is often found in sulfur dioxide, which is used in refrigeration and unfortunately is also a pollutant.

Speed-Building Practice

A draft or rough draft is any version of a document that is not in final form. Writing is really a thinking process, and few people know exactly what they want to say until after they have written the first draft. Then they see certain words they want to change, and they may think of details they want to add to the document. Most business writing goes through several quick drafts before it is complete. If you are composing your own materials or preparing documents for others, you will need to become skilled at working with corrections on rough drafts.

LESSON 29   Keyboarding Control

Warm-Up Practice
Second and Third Fingers

soon sort whose knows south course reasons resolve possible	12
I resolved, for some reason, to take a course to the south.	24
follow coal broad action cannot amount poorer through other	36
The long road cannot amount to much through the other town.	48

--1----2----3----4----5----6----7----8----9---10---11---12-

Fast-Paced Drill
Phrases and Sentences

since you can if that work is not all done could not try to	12
is this is finished are able to do so all the time if yours	24
Begin to gain control by keeping each finger moving evenly.	36
I am sure they will be on time; we must take more time now.	48

--1----2----3----4----5----6----7----8----9---10---11---12-

Warm-Up Practice
High-Frequency Sequences: Opposite Hands

```
ow to ck ig ua ry vi ov qu ur sh ne ti oc ek ob ld ic ro ty    12
her are any got ace has all get but one the you put led not    24
arts park part sort lark sons whom fail base what when sign    36
check there could first think count class bound might great    48
--1----2----3----4----5----6----7----8----9---10---11---12-
```

Fast-Paced Drill

```
Sixty words a minute is a good typing rate for most people.    12
If you do not want to be just average, climb up to seventy.    24
Typing at a good computer may push your speed up even more.    36
Almost anyone can make the rate faster by using the drills.    48
--1----2----3----4----5----6----7----8----9---10---11---12-
```

Attention Drill

```
    Many otherwise sensible people transform into complete     12
strangers in the office; these employees seem to enjoy each    24
chance to have an argument or disturb someone else.  Ignore    36
the temptation to get involved with those who like to argue    48
and remember that, in the office at least, there are always    60
better ways to solve a disagreement.  All employees want to    72
feel confident that their work is valued.  Often, those who    84
spend great amounts of time away from their desks feel that    96
they are not regarded as an essential part of the big team.   108
--1----2----3----4----5----6----7----8----9---10---11---12-
```

Speed-Building Practice

```
    The best way to gain skill in any field is to set your     12
goals high.  Sometimes there is no one around to direct the    24
effort, and you just have to make plans on your own.  Often    36
you can learn about a field by calling a school or library,    48
and now there are offices that provide you with information    60
or with phone numbers so you can call for information.  You    72
should remember that learning takes time.  Most people have    84
to allow several months or even years to make a change, but    96
those who keep their goals in mind will show up as winners.   108
--1----2----3----4----5----6----7----8----9---10---11---12-
```

Attention Drill

As soon as we found that the fish were obstructed from reaching the upper Penobscot Bay, we began to investigate methods to construct a fish ladder like that in use in Seattle since early 1992. The 20-foot drop in the water level, based on seasonal fluctuations, was a major impediment to progress in planning. However, the environmental engineering team of advisors from Woods Hole and local groups was able to devise a graduated system by which the fish can make their way to the traditional spawning grounds. See Figure 13-2 for details.

Speed-Building Practice

One of the problems with keying from clean copy is that the actual work to be done in an office is very seldom neat. You may have to read handwritten changes on a page of typed material. At other times you will be expected to look up words on your own, and sometimes you may have to check the commas or other marks in a letter. Right now you should focus on accuracy and speed, since those are the skills that will help you work quickly with every new project. Every practice section you key carefully now helps you develop the abilities you will need later.

LESSON 28	Keyboarding Control

Warm-Up Practice

Third Finger   kid loss load does solid dross swords learned worlds learns
The loss of this deal does not affect his record seriously.

Second Finger   red cede deed directed driven dinner friend turned confided
This direct knowledge of the deed increased our confidence.
--1----2----3----4----5----6----7----8----9---10---11---12-

Fast-Paced Drill

The embers formed a barrier that compelled our fast return.   12
I know that you will make a great success in your new work.   24
I want you to know about all our plans for this new school.   36
These arrangements that they made were entirely acceptable.   48
--1----2----3----4----5----6----7----8----9---10---11---12-

Warm-Up Practice: Frequent Letter Combinations

```
get ear day are ban bet not now was ton the one off let had    12
with will when what were well turn time this they them that    24
been fort come from have sent over send much know wing just    36
about after again close could count every going lease order    48
--1----2----3----4----5----6----7----8----9---10---11---12-
```

Fast-Paced Drill

```
It takes time to build skill.  We have to key drills daily.    12
They show their good character by their interest in others.    24
Please call us soon if we can be of help to you in any way.    36
We think we can send these notes to you as I did last year.    48
--1----2----3----4----5----6----7----8----9---10---11---12-
```

Attention Drill

```
     By December 1, 1999, the computer will be a fixture in     12
almost all businesses in the United States.  These powerful    24
devices have been taken from specialized technical settings    36
and placed in the offices of administrators, professionals,    48
executives, and self-employed people.  The passenger beside    60
you in an airplane may have a laptop computer with a simple    72
display screen.  Since the 1980s, companies have given much    84
investment in time and money to making computers accessible    96
for use by nontechnical staff.  Their effort has succeeded.   108
--1----2----3----4----5----6----7----8----9---10---11---12-
```

Speed-Building Practice

```
     No goal that is worth meeting can be reached without a     12
lot of work.  It is really true that those people who enjoy    24
their work are always the people who do good work.  You can    36
work hard on almost anything if your interest is strong.  A    48
good way to determine your own interests is to set aside an    60
hour or so every day to have some time for yourself.  There    72
is no reason to stay away from special courses and training    84
if you need more help to reach your goals.  Others are glad    96
to work with someone who wants to do the best possible job.   108
--1----2----3----4----5----6----7----8----9---10---11---12-
```

Attention Drill

An estuary is a body of water where salt water from the ocean, such as the Atlantic Ocean or Pacific Ocean, mixes with fresh water from the land; the animals and plants that inhabit these places are specially adapted for the estuary. Throughout the 1980s, efforts have been under way at the local, state, and federal level to protect these important bodies of water. Most of us would recognize the names of the largest estuaries because we have vacationed at one. In addition, many Americans actually live near estuaries such as Tampa Bay or San Francisco Bay.

Speed-Building Practice

Keyboarding is a skill that provides much professional, vocational, and personal value. Using the word processor or your typewriter for your correspondence could help make your letters easier for your friends to read. Strong handwriting is important, too, but most will agree that a typewritten or printed letter is a lot easier to read than a letter written in longhand. You may also save time because, with practice, you will keyboard much faster than you can write by hand. A big increase in demands on your time could convince you that typewriting skills are handy.

LESSON 27   Keyboarding Control

Warm-Up Practice

Home Row	Ask a glad lad all about an alfalfa salad made for his dad.
Upper Row	Quick typing would say quite a lot about our own good work.
Lower Row	Not very many zebras can be caged in zoos or by big fences.
Common Words	become copies didn't except accept compliment begin attempt
	--1----2----3----4----5----6----7----8----9---10---11---12-

Fast-Paced Drill

Many decisions are made on the basis of the educated guess.	12
The moon goes around the planet in approximately one month.	24
It is difficult to work with a person whose mind is closed.	36
More than once I have tried to learn how to do woodworking.	48
--1----2----3----4----5----6----7----8----9---10---11---12-	

Warm-Up Practice: High-Frequency Sequences

```
true prey kind much vent dear sigh sink idea make into line    12
air hen his oil law dig man elm fig met cob hat end for own    24
about shins press alike write sends steep finds feels books    36
it has this in any do not is in the is now we wish to offer    48
--1----2----3----4----5----6----7----8----9---10---11---12-
```

Fast-Paced Drill

```
If you work out a plan, be sure that you use the plan well.    12
You will build speed by using common sense and steady work.    24
When you read a book or newspaper, take some time to think.    36
It does take time to develop the ability to make decisions.    48
--1----2----3----4----5----6----7----8----9---10---11---12-
```

Attention Drill

```
    Most people find it difficult to follow directions and    12
to give directions to others.  As an example, try to decide    24
how you would show another employee how to operate your own    36
personal computer.  Perhaps you would say, "Before we begin    48
I will explain the computer to you."  You might instead ask    60
the person to simply turn on the switch, push a button, and    72
see what happens.  Those people who are accomplished at the    84
art of training others know how important it is to consider    96
the skill of the "student" and the need to feel successful.   108
--1----2----3----4----5----6----7----8----9---10---11---12-
```

Speed-Building Practice

```
    It is often difficult to decide when to attempt change    12
and when to simply accept things as they are.  Everyone can    24
name a person who is too much of an idealist and expects an    36
ideal world to take shape.  On the other hand, it would not    48
be hard to name a person who is against change on principle    60
and would benefit from hearing the voice of others who want    72
to make improvements.  It is certain that most people think    84
their interests are much more important than those of other    96
people.  Ideas should not be based only on selfish motives.   108
--1----2----3----4----5----6----7----8----9---10---11---12-
```

Attention Drill

Many businesses like the idea of putting plants in the office, and there is some reason to think this is a benefit to employees. (1) Many of us spend more time at work than we do in our own homes, and it is pleasant to see plants and flowers around the office. (2) More important, perhaps, is the fact that living plants absorb carbon dioxide and give off oxygen. Did you know that the material within plant cells is always in motion, as the plant carries out these natural operations? Some people have a hard time growing plants, but almost everyone likes them.

Speed-Building Practice

It is almost always a mistake to bring personal problems into the workplace. This good rule has stood for many years, but the rule is changing somewhat in the office of today. The fact is that many of us find it difficult to leave our private lives behind if we have children or other personal concerns outside the office. Outside concerns have an effect on your work, and most businesses now see the need to consider the many demands on their workers. Women and men with families may need time off if a family member is ill. Business is slowly adapting to such needs.

LESSON 26   Keyboarding Control

Warm-Up Practice
Combinations That Begin and End Words

```
by ty br ny de un gr em fy im ex ly ac ob en et em th ad al      12
sub ion ier ure thr pre con com ing ing ive ful ent ant ual     24
ambi diam ably ious ical tion tial fill able ible less sion     36
retro meter exact inco exact logic ation econo ician techno     48
--1----2----3----4----5----6----7----8----9---10---11---12-
```

Fast-Paced Drill

```
Our history teachers do the best they can in the classroom.     12
We heard many comments on the talks you gave to our groups.     24
A crazy dog herded six spotted sheep quickly over the edge.     36
Many feel loyalty for the college where they gained skills.     48
--1----2----3----4----5----6----7----8----9---10---11---12-
```

Warm-Up Practice: Frequent Letter Combinations

```
velvet letter little matter before return school should any    12
sight shall thank their there thing think which write wrote    24
state lance price other fancy thank azure noble since vogue    36
attention thought through enclose interest pleased pleasant    48
--1----2----3----4----5----6----7----8----9---10---11---12-
```

Fast-Paced Drill

```
Some people read books for fun and for the chance to think.    12
Once it got late, that manager went to the deli for snacks.    24
Terry found that the best paper is light white bond sheets.    36
The hazy sun was a problem for all planes taking off today.    48
--1----2----3----4----5----6----7----8----9---10---11---12-
```

Attention Drill

```
     Between 1990 and 1999, economies around the world will    12
be adjusting to the large-scale changes in military defense    24
and in political structures.  At present, no one can really    36
predict the long-range results of these changes.  One trend    48
that has emerged, however, is the greatly increased role of    60
citizens in helping to shape the future of their cities and    72
even their nation.  Those people who want the benefits of a    84
good society will no doubt begin to accept more of the work    96
of managing this structure and might have to work together.   108
--1----2----3----4----5----6----7----8----9---10---11---12-
```

Speed-Building Practice

```
     We say that things are changing rapidly in these times    12
we live in, and that statement is true.  If we just stop to    24
think, however, we see right away that almost all the major    36
change is taking place in general areas that many will call    48
unimportant.  The method for communication among people and    60
cooperation, and the need for generous attitudes, are still    72
the same as they were hundreds of years ago, long before an    84
electronic typewriter or a computer was found in almost any    96
office.  Things change, but people are often much the same.   108
--1----2----3----4----5----6----7----8----9---10---11---12-
```

End-of-Line Decisions

Up to now, the keyboarding control practice has been designed to end evenly at the right margin. For the remaining lessons in Level 2, you will make end-of-line decisions on your own.

The Warm-Up Practice and Fast-Paced Drill continue to end evenly. Key these lines exactly as shown. When you complete the Attention Drill and Speed-Building Practice, return whenever you reach the end of the line.

Computer-Users. Your instructor will probably want you to use your word processing word wrap feature. If so, use the pre-set margins and let the machine take care of line-ending decisions for you.

Hyphenating. Avoid hyphenating words at the end of the line. Many offices today prefer to allow an uneven right margin than to have employees spending a lot of time in reviewing the line breaks in a letter or other document.

Never hyphenate at the end of the line more than two times in a row. Too many hyphens at the right margin will make your document look choppy.

Warm-Up Practice
Syllable Keying

```
ty im en ac di ev ex ad fa ar so fi po al op un ap de im mo    12
ac id ev de al ob pa ma in do am go an to by wy on it is ew    24
bus lit aft nev com per con pre hav pro cer pos oth can sys    36
like ster semi hemi omni ideo mont deci vest cial deca teen    48
--1----2----3----4----5----6----7----8----9---10---11---12-
```

Fast-Paced Drill
Phrases and Sentences

```
That is true.  It may not be there.  I can try to be there.    12
I may have been too early.  They try to set high standards.    24
The way we spend our spare time shows much about ourselves.    36
Many efforts to bring change are hindered by lack of money.    48
--1----2----3----4----5----6----7----8----9---10---11---12-
```